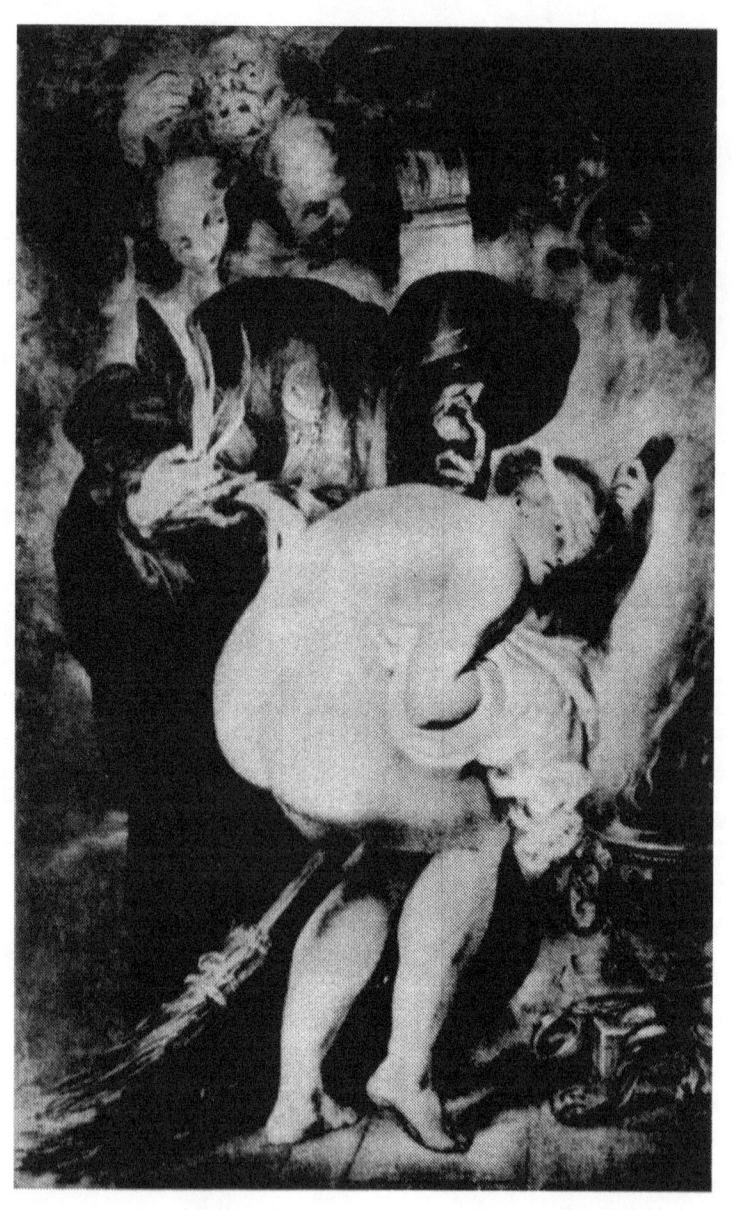

MAGICA SEXUALIS

MYSTIC LOVE BOOKS
OF BLACK ARTS AND
SECRET SCIENCES
By DR. EMILE LAURENT
AND PROF. PAUL NAGOUR

**Fredonia Books
Amsterdam, The Netherlands**

Magica Sexualis:
Mystic Love Books of Black Arts and Secret Sciences

by
Emile Laurent
Paul Nagour

ISBN: 1-4101-0425-7

Copyright © 2003 by Fredonia Books

Reprinted from the original edition

Fredonia Books
Amsterdam, The Netherlands
http://www.fredoniabooks.com

All rights reserved, including the right to reproduce this book, or portions thereof, in any form.

In order to make original editions of historical works available to scholars at an economical price, this facsimile of the original edition is reproduced from the best available copy and has been digitally enhanced to improve legibility, but the text remains unaltered to retain historical authenticity.

MAGICA SEXUALIS
MYSTIC LOVE BOOKS
OF
BLACK MAGIC
AND
SECRET SCIENCES

MEPHISTOPHELES

    Make only the engagement, and at once
    All will be pleasure—I have rare devices
    And my craft will show thee many marvels
    Right strange and merry scenes will conjure up;
    Sights shalt thou see that man hath never seen.

GOETHE'S Faust

FAUST

    This senseless witchcraft sickens and disgusts me—
    And sayest thou that I shall recruit life's powers,
    Here in this loathsome den of filthy madness?
    Shall I petition an old hag for counsel?
    And can the nauseous puddle of the pot
    Make me a younger man by thirty winters?
    Is there in Nature no restorative
    But this? Has Spirit never yet devised
    Means different to restore the springs of life?

                                                            GOETHE'S *Faust*

CONTENTS

INTRODUCTION

PAGE

Universality and Eternity of Sexual Magic......... 1

CHAPTER 1
Sex in the World of Magic

§ 1. *White and Black Magic—Sexual Occultism*........ 9
§ 2. *The Cabala*..13
§ 3. *Love of Angels for Women*..........................17
§ 4. *Angels as Divine Ambassadors of Love—Dusii—Evil Angels*..18
§ 5. *The Devachan—State of Theosophic Love*...........20
§ 6. *The Hermetic Essence and Alchemy*..................22
§ 7. *Astrology: Enormous Influence on Amours*........24
§ 8. *Spiritualism and Modern Secret Science*...............25

CHAPTER 2
Satanism and Demon Worship—
Erotico-Mystic Perversions

§ 1. *Demonomania and Human Sexuality*....................29
§ 2. *Satan's Powers in the Province of Sex—44,435,556 Devils* 30
§ 3. *Cult of the Demons—Its Sacrelegious Ceremonials* 33

CHAPTER 3
Incubi and Succubi

§ 1. *Demoniac Possession*...38
§ 2. *Copulations of the Incubi—Authentic Documents*..39
§ 3. *Immoral Mysteries of the Succubus*....................47
§ 4. *Interpretations of the Incubus*..............................49

CHAPTER 4
The Devil's Copulations

               PAGE

§ 1. *The Devil's Contract: Eleven Vilifying Ceremonials* 52
§ 2. *The Spawn of the Devil: Illustrious Offspring*........55
§ 3. *Magic Erotic Physiology of the Devil: "Sons of God with the Daughters of men": Giant Births*..57

CHAPTER 5
The Witches' Sabbath

§ 1. *How the Witches' Sabbath Came About: Secret Assemblies*..63
§ 2. *The Witches' Ride: The Witches' Aphrodisiac Salve* 66
§ 3. *Bestial Ceremonies of the Witches' Sabbath—Satan's Chamber-pot*..72

CHAPTER 6
The Black Mass and Its Orgies

§ 1. *The Cult of the Manicheans—Black Mass in the Middle Ages*..75
§ 2. *Triumph of the Black Mass in the Century of Louis XIV.—Abominable Proceedings—Voisin; Marquise de Montespan — Magical Aphrodisiac Pills* 77
§ 3. *Modern Societies for the Celebration of Satanism: Re-Theurgistes Optimates*..................................81
§ 4. *The Best and Most Striking Account of a Black Mass by a Great Contemporary Frenchman who Was an Eyewitness: the Shuddering Rituals*......83

CHAPTER 7

Werewolves and Vampires

PAGE
§ 1. *Werewolves—Lycanthropy for Sexual Sin*............96
§ 2. *Vampirism* 98

CHAPTER 8

Sex Enchantments

§ 1. *Amatory Witchcraft—Ancient Love enchantments*.102
§ 2. *Workings of Magical Operations—A Valuable Document of the Middle Ages—Case of Bishop Guichard—His Confessions—His Magical Methods of Causing Love in Others*............................104
§ 3. *Mystic Methods to Win the Love of a Man or a Woman* 107
§ 4. *Enchantments by Means of Photographs*............109
§ 5. *Modern Magic Formulas—Love-drinks, Flesh, Talismans, Love-inks* 110
§ 6. *Danger of Enchantments*................................112
§ 7. *Strange Case of Gaufridi—Seduction of women by his breath—Prince of Magicians burnt in public*..113
§ 8. *Case of Urbain Grandier—His Phenomenal Power Over Women*..115
§ 9. *Erotic Fascination—Modern Cases—Case of Castellan—His Hypnotic Fascination of Women—Mme. Chambige's Tragic Enchantment—Case of Henry Prince: A Bold Public Exhibition of Physical Fascination!*..117

CHAPTER 9

Magic Drinks — Magic Invocations Magic Aphrodisiacs

	PAGE
§ 1. Love-charms of the Egyptians	123
§ 2. Invocations Among the Arabians and Greeks	124
§ 3. Inseparability of Magic and Love—How to Win Back Lost Love	126
§ 4. Compounding of Aphrodisiac Magic Drinks—Modern Opotherapy—Old Man Young Again—Old Woman Young Again	129
§ 5. Hindu Love-charms—Magical Pharmacopœia—Conquest of Women—Magic Drinks for Increasing Sexual Vigor—Miraculous Aphrodisiacs in Magic Book of Albertus Magnus	132
§ 6. Human Blood and the Witchcraft of Love	139
§ 7. Magical Love-Philtres and Talismans Against Impotency	141

CHAPTER 10

Sex Talismans and Amulets

§ 1. Phallic Talismans of Classical and Medieval Times	145
§ 2. Modern Erotic Talismans—Astrology and Secret Properties of Jewels	146
§ 3. Classifications of Talismans	149
§ 4. Talismanic Formulas of the Magic Books—Their Wondrous Rôle in Love and Sex	151
§ 5. Symbolic Jewelry	154
§ 6. Phallic Monuments in Ireland, United States, India—Amatory Pilgrimages	156

§ 7. *Metals Sacred to Venus—Arabian Love-magnet*..157
§ 8. *Secret Properties of Gems in Province of Sex— Stones and Sins—Natural Magic*..........................159
§ 9. *Mandrake or Mandragora, "the Human-bodied"— Morion or Death-wine Administered to the Crucified—Babylonian Charm Against Sterility*........163
§10. *Astrologic Talismans—The Planet of Love*........165
§ 11. *Cryptic Letters and Numbers — The Seven Talismans of King Solomon—Magic Tables of Sex*....167
§12. *Practical Power of Belief in Talismans*.................170

CHAPTER 11
Sex Languages and Symbols
§ 1. *The Language of Flowers — Charts*....................172
§ 2. *The Flower-clock for Rendezvous of Lovers*........175
§ 3. *Plants and Flowers of Love—Pumpkins and Pomgranates in the Cult of Venus—The Rose*............176
§ 4. *The Language of Stamps—Hidden code of lovers*..177
§ 5. *The Science of Auguries and Premonitions*........179
§ 6. *The Science of Prophesying—A Myriad Branches*..180
§ 7. *Days Favorable to Fertility in Women*................184
§ 8. *The Planet Venus—Sexual Side of Astrology*....185

CHAPTER 12
Dreams and Sexual Magic
§ 1. *Pleasures in Dreams*...189
§ 2. *Joys of Love in Dreams—Hashish*....................190
§ 3. *Methods of Interpretation of Dreams—Oriental Systems — Freudian Sex Interpretations*...........192
§ 4. *Freudian Cases* 194
§ 5. *Sexual Symbolism in Dreams*..........................196
§ 6. *The Magic Art of Creating Erotic Dreams*..........198

CHAPTER 13

Sexual Music and Sexual Dances in the Orient and Occident

PAGE

§ 1. Sexual Influence of Music — The Food of Love — The Mad Love of Demetrius Polyorketes for the Courtesan Lamia..................201

§ 2. Pages of Sex in Music—Sex Permeates Music of Gounod—Sexual Exaltation in Wagner's Music—Triumphant Erotic Music of Berlioz—Perversions and Music..................204

§ 3. Sexual Dances—Seduction of the Courtesans—Erotic Dances of the Daughters of the Ouled-Naïl 207

CHAPTER 14
Christianity and Sexual Magic

§ 1. Christianity and Sex—The Prohibitions of the Father Confessors and the Church Fathers—Their Wise and Unwise Sexual Precepts—The Denial of the Great Law of Sex—Religious Erotomania 212

§ 2. The Reaction—The Erotico-religious Perversions..222

CHAPTER 15
Mystical Sexual Miscellanies

§ 1. Ecstasy and Sex..................226

§ 2. Magical Powers of Virginal Perspiration (Odor di Femina)—Sunamitism—Elixir for Lengthening Man's Life..................228

§ 3. Osphresiological Love Charms..................233

§ 4. *Medieval Love Courts — Rehabilitation of Love and Sex from Degradation by Moralizers — Princesses as Instructresses in Science of Love — Sixty Female Counsellors — Bold Laws and Dicta of the Codex of Love*..................235

CHAPTER 16
Mystic Philosophy of Copulation Through the Ages

§ 1. *Sex, the Law of the Universe*..................242
§ 2. *Immemorial Conceptions of Sex — Vedic Love in India — Descriptions of Festivals of the Lingam and Phallus*..................243
§ 3. *Zoroaster and Prayer to Purify Act of Love*..................249
§ 4. *Sex in the Chaldean Religions*..................250
§ 5. *Sex in the Assyrian Religions — Priests of Baal*....251
§ 6. *Sex and the Religions of Egypt — Isis Festivals*....252
§ 7. *Cult of the Phallus — Dionysian Festivals — Cult of Cotytto and Nymphomania*..................253
§ 8. *The Corybantes — Cult of Priapus in Rome*..................256
§ 9. *Cult of Venus — Spiritual Union and the Goddess of Sex*..................259
§10. *Sex in the Religions of Nordic Countries*..................262
§11. *Islam and Sex — Adoration of Sex — Sex-Act as Form of Prayer*..................264
§12. *Sex as Mistress of the World — Sex the Most Amazing Miracle of All Time*..................267
Bibliography..................269
Cabinet of Unusual Illustrations..................275

INTRODUCTION

INTRODUCTION

Universality and Eternity
of Sexual Magic

MAGICA SEXUALIS! It predestinates man and his universe. It is a basic law in the mind of man and at the same time the weirdest of all the mysteries of the universe. In some form or other Black Magic and Erotic Occultism are to be found in all the fleeting pages of history. Let us here cast but a quick glance at three indigenous stages in the development of mankind.

First, among the ancient South American *Kali-kans*. Horrified cries break out among the aborigines as they chance to discover a black spot gradually growing in the sky and blotting out their life-giving sun. The tribal chief immediately hurls imprecations at the *devil*. Then, in turn, supplications. But his word-magic fails. Quickly the aborigines start beating their tom-toms. But their sun is already three-fourths demolished. Their music-magic has failed. They finally resort to the quick-sacrifice of a young virgin. The sun is completely extinguished as the crude stone-hammer of the chief mightily smashes out the brains of the innocent victim. This virginal sacrifice, the most potent art of magic, has finally appeased the malignant devil who releases the sun from his bondage and allows it to shine on a thoroughly chastened world.

The scene changes. Any continental country, including England and the Americas. The time: from the twelfth century through the Middle Ages, up to 1823 in England and to 1807 in the United States. We are in the midst of a typical inquisition. At the bench sit seven learned judges; before them stand an array of women, ranging from beautiful young virgins to withered hags and crones. The clerk intones the charges against them: "Janet Lee, you are accused of the heinous crime of copulating with the demon Satan . . . Mary Stanton, you are accused of riding off into the skies to the witches' sabbath and of there participating in such hideous practices as pressing your lips on the genital parts of the presiding devil, not forgetting the sacrilegious imprint of your lips on the foul creature's buttocks . . . Susan Graham, you are accused of participating in a Black Mass and of mixing human semen and excrements to the sacred Host. . . ." Thus the list goes on, heaping erotic mania on criminal profanations. But

Introduction

the most amazing part is that the accused women confess to these sins and plead guilty to even stranger charges! Indeed, the accused women often gave detailed accounts of their copulations with the devil! Their stories, as well as the reasons underlying them, will be given in complete form in their proper place in the book.

The scene again changes. We are in Paris, some time before the World War. In a crooked street in a suburb of Paris a strange meeting is taking place in a deserted chapel. In front of the statues of the saints, against which barren women were wont to rub their pudenda in order to ensure offspring, a low mass is being celebrated by a priest who specialized in seducing the pretty girls who came to him for confessional. But this mass is of a peculiar nature. It is not consecrated to the Lord of Heaven but to the Prince of Darkness; not to God and all that is good, but to the Devil and all that is evil. A Black Mass is being performed, with all its obscene rites and ghastly ceremonies.

Magica Sexualis! It knows no time, no clime. It is as mysterious today as in unremembered Chaldea, and as cryptic as the Sphinx. Here you will find alchemic symbols, talismanic characters, bizarre pentacles, crosses and stars, and a host of other enigmatic matters that will cause the reader to ponder over the actual length and breadth of sexual magic in everyday life. For sex is magic, and magic is sex. Star dust is composed of particles of sex and there is magic in the eroticism of men and women. One supposes and presupposes the other. As there can be no light if there are no eyes to see, so there can be no sex without magic in it. What draws man to woman? What pulls one planet to another? What turns and twirls this earth of ours and all the creatures on it?

DR. ÉMILE LAURENT
PROF. PAUL NAGOUR

MAGICA SEXUALIS
MYSTIC LOVE BOOKS
of BLACK MAGIC *and* SECRET SCIENCES

MAGICA SEXUALIS
MYSTIC LOVE BOOKS
of BLACK MAGIC *and* SECRET SCIENCES

CHAPTER ONE
SEX IN THE WORLD OF MAGIC

§ 1
WHITE AND BLACK MAGIC
SEXUAL OCCULTISM

WE intend to examine in this handbook of sexual magic the mystic phenomena of all that pertains to love and woman, with particular emphasis on black magic. Sexual occultism is a generic term, replete with abstruse ambiguities, and for our purpose therefore we employ the more satisfactory term, sexual magic.

The genuine esoteric meaning of magic is the knowledge of the principle and means by which the omniscience and omnipotence of the spirit, combined with power over matter, can be acquired from living individuals. In order to procure this omniscience and omnipotence, adepts of all times and places have studiously cultivated various branches of this mystic, secretive science. Let us present a brief summation of these various branches.

Theurgy, or white magic, is the science of procuring divine or supernatural intervention in human affairs, especially with beneficent results. This science was widely practiced by the Egyptian Neo-Platonists, particularly Plotinus, Porphyrius, Iamblichus, and Julian Apostata.

The theurgists believed only in white magic, and in the invocation of beneficent demons or angels in order to do good for mankind. Contrarily, goëty is the invocation of maleficent spirits for the purpose of working evil on humanity.

Theurgy concerns itself with the preparation of amulets, talismans and of all other wondrous panaceas that call forth the heavenly powers as aids. This branch of magic has been employed by the earliest heathens no less than by modern religions. Instead of the multitude of beneficent deities of the ancients, we now have the miracle-working angels, saints, spirits, fairies, etc. Their secret symbols are known and shown in their practical applications in the Cabala.

"The theurgists," says Bonnamy, "attributed divine power to their symbols and ceremonies, with which they believed themselves enclothed. Ancient heroes, like Jason, Castor, Pollux and Hercules had but to record the results of miracles for they were full-fledged initiates."

White magic commonly combines mind-reading, secret-writing, the symbolic meanings of flowers, metals, colors, etc., certain mathematical combinations, and many another esoteric mystery of the visible and invisible world. Incomplete as this handbook of sexual magic may be, it will nevertheless surprise many readers who previously have had no suspicion of their magical powers and who have unconsciously practiced white magic.

Theurgy consists almost solely of simple doctrines and symbolisms. The unitiated may watch the pretty young woman closely at the dinner table, but will be unaware that she has made a rendezvous with her lover for tomorrow afternoon, five o'clock, street number and apartment, if the significance of the bouquet of flowers carelessly left on the table has escaped their notice; even a certain arrangement of clothing, hair, gloves, hat, etc., may each have a definite significance.

Such initiates might read a long letter of four or five pages without receiving any impressions other than the general meaning of its contents; but the initiate will without any difficulty read between the lines and understand the hidden meaning. One needs but to read the Greek and Latin poets to be thoroughly convinced of how these magical stratagems have been enlisted in the field of sex, and to be astounded at their subtle efficacy.

Lovers ever and everywhere have instinctively turned to these esoteric methods to learn their fate, increase their power, carry out clandestine love affairs, and accomplish numerous other ends impossible otherwise.

Goëty, or black magic, is the science of procuring the intervention of the devil in human affairs for evil purposes. Marquardt in his *Roman Cults* describes its chief purposes: to inflict evil on the good; to harm persons by producing sickness, madness or death; to seduce men and women by magic potions; to prophesy the future by invocation of the dead and exorcism of evil spirits; to make gold by adjuring the avenging spirits, etc.

The masters of the fantastic in literature and art find that their most horrifying works are but poor and naïve terrors compared to the formulas and doctrines found in books on black magic. From the very first pages the reader experiences a certain disquiet and nausea. The impression received is quite similar to that a sensitive person would feel if he had breakfast in a dissecting room. The horrible odors of an abattoir combine with the pungent stench of an unclean pharmacopœia and the smell of violated graces.

Black magic directs the magician in his criminal transactions; it directs the witches' sabbath; it presides in enchantments, in secret crimes. Its code is horrifying; its arsenal: poisonous flowers and plants, diseased animals, bones of the dead, adipocere, and the skin of executed persons. All its transactions take place in lurid darkness, at the witching hour of midnight, preferably in the very foulest weather when rain and wind are raging.

Its devotees delight in transacting their sinister business in grottoes, caves, churchyards, ruins, old castles; and such dismal places as the gallows-yard. At times they hide themselves in the shadows of the woods, and hold their assemblies on some crossroad that has attained local notoriety by some inexplicable assassination.

The associates of goëty are even more revolting. To

this group belong demons, spectres, nocturnal ghosts, vampires, necrophiliac beings, incubi and succubi, in short, all the nightmarish chimeræ of ghastly fears, rites and superstitions.

§ 2

THE CABALA

The Cabala — the word literally signifies tradition — embraces the entirety of esoteric theories. It is, so to speak, the bible of secret sciences and sexual mysteries. Every word, every phrase, of this cryptic bible can be interpreted in no less than three ways: literal, figurative and esoteric.

It is obvious that not everyone is privileged to read the Cabala. Moreover, it is written in Hebraic, and only an expert Hebraist is able to read it. Accordingly, only a few adepts of the black arts and secret sciences are able to pierce the veil of the inscrutable centuries and master this traditional key to the ages.

According to the rabbis, the Cabala was transmitted hand to hand from Adam to Moses, and it was only by the aid of these formulas that the great thaumaturgist was able to achieve the miracles ascribed to him. In fact, in recapitulating the miracles of Moses, they will be found very similar to those of Hindu fakirs and Brahmans: levitation of the body, materialization of the spirit, the immediate growth of certain flowers and plants, meteorological phenomena, etc.

The rabbis and the Indian occultists possess the key to the Cabala. Whereas the former merely possess the knowledge of the formulas, the latter understand its esoteric significance. In point of sagacity, certain of these formulas are, to say the least, most extraordinary:

Thus it contains the following mystic doctrines:

1. A combination of letters meaningless to the uninitiate
2. The restoration of an historic event in the form of a rebus
3. An alchemistic formula
4. A philosophic concept

De la Mauze explains that there are three-letter combinations in the Cabala. "The first," he says, "is the transposal of the letters of a word into another word consisting of the same letters, forming an anagram. The second consists in taking the letters of a word and forming many different words from the initial letters, thus making an acrostic. The third consists in exchanging the letters of a word for other letters in a logical and systematic fashion, a kind of secret writing."

Thus, according to Stanislaus de Guaita, the key that opened the grave of Hiram — symbol of the synthetic theory of the ancients—was found in the hieroglyphic

The Cabala

formula of the divine tetragram: *Iod-Heve=Jehova*, which correspond to the cabalistic letters, containing *iod*, *he*, *vau*, and *he*.

Iod is the masculine spirit, the active creative principle, *deus in se*, the good. It embraces the phallic symbol, the sceptre of Tarok and the columns of Iakin in the temple of Solomon. In alchemy it is represented by sulphur.

He is the passive substance, the feminine productive principle, the formative world spirit, the potency of evil, figuratively represented by Cteis, the libational vessel of Tarok and the columns of Boaz. In alchemy it is quicksilver.

Vau is the fructifying combination of both principles, the divine copulation, the eternal being, figuratively represented by the lingam, the winged staff and the sword of Tarok. In alchemy it is azoth, the mercury of the sages.

He is the fruitfulness of nature in the visible world, the last transformation of thought into visible forms, the shekel of Tarok.

The rhapsodist Orpheus, initiate of the divinities of Thebes and sacrificial priest to the great Zeus, was able, by means of the soulful songs from his seven-stringed lyre, to move stones. These he activated by the magnetism of his voice, which also brought the savage animals to tears, and made the ancient rugged oaks tremble with love.

Jesus of Nazareth, Apollonius of Tion were well

acquainted with the esoteric theosophy handed down from generation to generation since Moses and contained in the two books of the Cabala, in the Sepher-Jezirah and in the Zohar.

In a word, the operations of this science, as De la Mauze explains, essentially turn on a definite system and decided form of Hebraic letters, the distinction between straight or crooked, horizontal or vertical lines, down to the commas and periods of punctuation. "This form of the characters," he says, "rules the explanation of the names of God and the angels, the thirty-two ways of wisdom and the fifty gates of justice, which form the unchangeable basis of the Cabala."

"From the dogmatic standpoint," says Prost, "the Cabala contains a combination of badly digested theories, governed by the chief principle of emanation; masses of completely confusing concepts in relation to the spirit and its classification, the souls, geniuses, angels and demons; all this in the framework of a theosophy which has been perverted with oriental impregnation."

Thus the Cabala has become a pot-pourri of a thousand and one creations of supernatural beings, and has borrowed the superstitious beliefs of all countries. In the middle ages it underwent a number of changes and divided itself into branches: the Christian Cabala, the magic Cabala, the theoretical Cabala (iyyunith), the practical Cabala (maasith), etc.

§ 3

LOVE OF ANGELS FOR WOMEN

Cabalists and other occultists believe that both beneficent and maleficent spirits find pleasure in mundane sexuality. Many mystics believe that the angels of God also have the human failing of finding pleasure in the fruits of woman.

According to the book of Henoch in the *Apocrypha*, the angels took on the form of human beings and had intercourse with the wives and daughters of man. This notion was so firmly believed in the first century of Christianity that St. Justinus, Athenagores, Lactantius, Tertullian, and others reported such acts as beyond doubt.

Bizouard very logically notes that "the copulation of angels with women was so generally recognized that the births of important persons of the Middle Ages were ascribed to them, and the more reasonable men of later centuries did not know what to make of the whole affair."

Even St. Augustine dared not speak out against these beliefs, and St. Thomas Aquinas recognized that "the angel is a spiritual being. Although it is incorporeal in relation to us, it is corporeal in relation to God. At times angels assume a body in order to have intercourse with man. He represents to them neither a driving power nor a form in union; he is simply an emanation of the divine will. The angels walk and talk like living men although they are of a diviner nature."

§ 4

Angels as Divine Ambassadors of Love

Dusii — Evil Angels

The Cabala grants a significant rôle to the angels. It contains a list of seventy-two angels with whose help man can rise over the common world and work miracles. These angels have their definite authority and privileges and each of them stands in some special relation to one of the seven planets or one of the four quarters of heaven. They have their stars, their numbers, their days, and their special fragrances.

The angels of Venus, the divine ambassadors of love, are called Aniel and Anaël and reside in the Occident. The spirit of Venus, spirit of the heavenly being, is called Haegit and resides in the Orient. Friday is the day devoted to the Queen of Love according to tradition and hence the angels of this day naturally favor lovers. These are Rachiel and Sachiel, lieutenants of the already named Anaël. The "ruling angel of the air" is

King Sarabotes; king, since there are classes among the angels as there are among the demons. Servants of King Sarabotes are Amabiel, Aba, Abalidot and Flaef.

Next to the good angels in this world are the evil angels, who are nevertheless not counted as belonging to the demons. To this number belongs Isheth Zemunin, the angel of prostitution and wife of Samael, angel of poison and death.

The Cabala also admits four elementary spirits who correspond to the four elements: the sylphs for the air, the salamanders for fire, the undines for water, and the gnomes for the earth.

The Middle Ages also peopled the forests and plains with angels, sylphs, fairies, elves and the like. They are blessed, or cursed, with the same erotic inclinations by which the Greeks and Romans characterized their gods. Such were the *dusii* of the Gauls, a class of incubi who delighted in making cuckolds of virtuous husbands, and the field maidens of the twelfth century who, the legend goes, would appear to the dying peasants and would mock them with erotic temptations.

Paracelsus boldly writes: "Not only did people see nymphs, but they would even speak to them and would often have carnal connection with them."

The *Dictionnaire infernal* reports the adventure of a young Bavarian nobleman who was left inconsolable by the death of his young wife. A sylph assumed the form of the deceased and thus appeared to the young man, saying that God had received her in order to console him in his deep sorrow. They lived for many years together very happily, but upon an affront to her she suddenly disappeared forever.

St. Augustine is completely convinced of the existence of these creatures. "It is a well-known fact," he asserts, "and many have learnt it from persons whose honesty and faith cannot be questioned. The forest-gods, the satyrs and fawns, usually called incubi, often plague women and satisfy their passion upon them. Moreover, many noble persons have averred that there are demons called dusii by the Gauls, who practice such abominations on women every day in the year."

§ 5

THE DEVACHAN

STATE OF THEOSOPHIC LOVE

Mystic theosophy also believes in a kind of pure and passionate love which holds in readiness for its epopts when they are desirous of obtaining the state of the *devachan*.

"The devachan," says Jules Lermina in his *Magie pratique*, "is a transitive stage, in some measure a state of quietude, out of which the individual withdraws after a long stay. It has absolute freedom to become a new man and to continue the work of its purification in order

The Devachan

to quicken its eventual return to Nirvana where it will again become identical with the original spiritual principle."

This middle stage lies somewhere between purgatory and the paradise of Mohammed. The *Revue théosophique* reports on how love and sex are there conceived: "Although the state of the devachan is inseparable from the sensations and purely sensual inclinations of the last personality, it does not follow that the thoughts and aspirations of a metaphysical character persevere in this new state.

"On the contrary! All the sensations proceeding from a higher plane find their sphere of development in the devachan. All that we have dreamed of, if our dreams were justified and of a sublime character, are there realized. All those whom we have embraced with tender and passionate love are there to meet us and always to remain with us."

Lermina reinforces this view with even more definite statements and clearer expressions. "The devachan," he further suggests, "is the creative power, presenting the beloved image next to that of the lover, desirous of her presence and always prepared to satisfy the slightest desire of the beloved being. The one thing lacking there is that which corresponds to a physical sexual union, a material body or *mayavi-rupa*, an illusionary body which is just as invisible to the spiritual senses as the spiritual body is to the physical. If two beings love one another and only one attains the state of the devachan, then the one left on earth can have the sensations of the lover only in dreams while the devachan personality enjoys the beloved all the time."

§ 6

THE HERMETIC ESSENCE

AND ALCHEMY

According to some writers, the hermetic science came from Egypt and was discovered by Hermes Trismegistus or the god Thoth, who handed on the secrets of alchemy to the priests of Thebes and Memphis. According to others, alchemy was cultivated in the schools of Babylonian magic; still others assert that it was known in the most ancient times and that the Chinese knew of it at least two-thousand five-hundred years before the birth of Christ.

The alchemist sought "the philosophers' stone," a powder which would transform mercury and lead into gold. This powder was, at the same time, a kind of elixir of life, since it formed a mighty agent for the purifying of blood; it would have a similar effect on plants, and in the course of a few hours, they would grow, ripen and bear fruit. In a word all the virtues of the philosophers' stone were directed to the increase in the activity of life. It was to be an universal panacea.

The laboratories of the alchemists were hidden and concealed places erected under the protection of the Almighty. Their apparatus was of symbolic and bizarre forms; the oven in the form of a woman's womb was reminiscent of the production of metal, the image for which is woman, in whose womb pregnancy takes place.

Alchemy had its charlatans, but modern science has been just as unable to prevent tricksters from entering the field of scientific investigation. At any rate we can now say that alchemy was no idle dream, no chimera. Rubies and pearls are now made in the laboratories and are sold to the public. Base metals have been converted into gold, though at present only in slight quantity and at great cost. But there is no scientific reason why the philosophers' stone should not become an actuality and for the transmutation of metals to become a commonplace. We are unable at present to hazard a guess at possible physical benefits of such processes but it is not to be doubted that when we are able to change the atomic structure of elements at will, great advances will have been made in our knowledge of the human body.

§ 7

ASTROLOGY

ITS ENORMOUS INFLUENCE ON AMOURS

Astrology was formerly the science of prophecy *par excellence*. The magicians of Chaldea, its native land, questioned the heavens like some immense book, in which every star received a name and a significance from one of the letters of the Hebrew alphabet. It interpreted the fates of kings, men and empires, since all were subjected to the influence of the planets. The Jew, Simeon ben Bochai, to whom the authorship of the famous book *Zohar* is ascribed, according to talmudic legend, acquired so absolute a knowledge of the secrets of heaven that he could read the laws of Jehovah before they were even promulgated on earth.

According to this theory all lands, animals and plants were under the power of the celestial bodies.

The seven planets known to the ancients and the twelve signs of the animal kingdom formed the elements of the system. Each planet, each constellation, governed a certain part of the body, or a man, a kingdom, a city or a day.

The influence of the celestial bodies on the amours and intrigues of the heart was enormous; all astrology

Spiritualism

rested on the art of controlling these influences for the needs of love-adventures, ambition and happiness.

§ 8

Spiritualism
and
Modern Secret Science

Spiritualism is one of the modern forms of occultism and of the black arts and secret sciences, and can point to an enormous number of adherents and believers at the present time. It includes in its flock scientists and sages as well as peasants and panders. Is it just pure charlatanry, a pleasant illusion, or the realization of unknown phenomena, for which we entirely lack an explanation? Death, the inexorable and pitiless, is it but a release, the separation of the liberated spirit from the biologic matter? Or is death actually the final destruction, a total annihilation against the resurrection of a new life in the morning sun? Does death lead to the total darkness of the night or does it bring the vaunted light to the souls eagerly searching for the portals of eternal life?

Such problems have anxiously engaged all persons who have been tormented by the riddle of the beyond.

Let us see what the spiritualists teach in this regard.

According to Allen-Kardec, the soul is the intelligent

principle *per se*; it is the thinking power which we can conceive of only as an abstraction when isolated from matter. With its liquid frame or when enclosed in the ectoplasm, the soul designates the being which is called spirit, with its corporeal cover towards man. Although in its state as spirit it possesses especial properties and potencies, it has not ceased to belong to human nature. The spirits are hence beings similar to us, since each one of us becomes a spirit after the death of his body, and each spirit becomes a man by birth.

But, adds Delanne, the soul possesses the ectoplasmic cover not merely in its state as spirit, but that it is inseparable from this cover. During the human life the ectoplasmic fluid identifies itself with the body and serves as a vehicle for the external impressions and temperaments of the spirit; it permeates the body in all its parts; but at death the ectoplasm, together with the soul with which it shares the immortality, becomes free.

This theory therefore permits the eternality of the soul and the wanderings in the unknown worlds, planets and suns that gravitate in space.

Besides its corporeal cover, called body, the immaterial soul (*psyche anima*) possesses a second cover (*nous, spiritus*), the ectoplasm, which is not immaterial. Ectoplasm is formed of fluids of varying degrees of consistency, from the material fluids that cling to the brain to the spiritual fluids whose nature approaches that of the soul (soul-substance).

Spiritualism

Thus the soul and its fluidic cover, ectoplasm, form what the spiritualists call spirits.

At our death this spirit leaves our body and, according to whether our life was good or bad, ascends to the upper worlds or enters a new period of trial on earth.

Only when the spirit is completely dematerialized, declares Delanne, do the earlier lives unfold before it. Then only does it recall its last existence, and all the events that took place before it are as an immense panorama depicted before its eyes. It considers the advances that it has made as well as the advances it has still to make, and in this fashion does the desire seize it to incorporate itself anew so that it may more quickly attain that blessed world for which it longs.

On certain solemn occasions it can however by means of its will, as the spiritualists teach, change the nature of its fluidic frame and make itself visible for a short period of time, and indeed under its previous form in life. That is the spiritualistic theory of manifestations.

By means of the ectoplasm the spirit can make itself felt by the execution of physical phenomena, such as table-rapping, levitation, slate-writing, moving of furniture, etc. By this are to be explained the phenomena of the dancing tables, haunted-houses, etc.

If the puzzles of this belief are to be credited then those who wish to experiment with spiritualism should be warned that it is dangerous to traffic with ghosts. Delanne assures us that every question put to the spirits from a purely egoistic standpoint or from mere merriment will not only not be answered but may even cause the questioner to undergo physical as well as mental torture. Paul Gibier tells of many strange occurrences that befell him and his mediums and warns of the greatest caution.

From the religious standpoint adds Allen-Kardec, spiritualism has as a basis the fundamental verities of all religions: God, soul, immortality, future rewards and punishments; but it is independent of any one religion.

CHAPTER TWO

SATANISM AND DEMON-WORSHIP EROTICO-MYSTIC PERVERSIONS

§ 1

DEMONOMANIA AND HUMAN SEXUALITY

Plotinus has declared in the *Enneads* that the celestial bodies are acquainted with our desires and that demons possess both memory and mind and are hence responsive to those who entreat them. Berthelot confirms these hypotheses, or better, this attitude, in his study of the magic papyri of the Greeks. St. Cyprian on his part says: "There are evil and restless spirits who have obliterated all the beauty of their birth in the filth of the world. After they have lost all the excellences of their nature by having been steeped in vice they seek to console themselves by thrusting everybody else into the same grime and filth." Bodin specifies their power more clearly: "All Hebrews are at one," he says, "in believing that the devil, as a result of divine permission, possesses great power over the genital organs and lustfulness."

Teachers of demonomania who have seen so many companions of Satan in Jupiter, Vulcan, Apollo and other divinities of pagan days, say quite seriously that Pan was the first of the incubi or of those demons who cohabited with women. Lilith on the other hand was the leader or princess of the succubi or those demons who cohabited with men.

§ 2

SATAN'S POWERS IN THE PROVINCE OF SEX

44,435,556 DEVILS

Theurgy invokes the angels to attain its purposes and goëty similarly turns to the demons. The masters of the occult art of the middle ages even assure us that it was completely necessary to have recourse to these means in all magical operations. In order for these operations to succeed one must, according to Louandre's *Sorcellerie,* name all the demons. This naturally leads to confusion for it is very difficult to know all the subjects of this infernal monarchy, as the demonographists call themselves.

However, we can make the following recapitulation:

1. Beelzebub, emperor of the legion of the devil.
2. The 7 kingdoms: Bael, Pursen, Byleth, Paymon, Belial, Asmodeus, Zapan. These rule the 4 parts of heaven
3. 23 dukes, 10 counts, 11 presidents, and 100 knights.
4. 6,666 legions, each formed of 6,666 devils. Hence, altogether 44,435,556 devils.

From this table can be ascertained the enormous amount of time required for even the very smallest magical operations; in addition, the chances of its failure were very great. But a single mistake in naming this rather large list of devils would nullify all the labor already done. In order to remedy this evil state of affairs, the old cabalists prepared their famous magic books, of which we shall speak later.

In relation to demons and their attributes there can be found the most curious and most detailed accounts in Collin de Plancy's *Dictionnaire infernal*. If the author does not give a complete number of these notorious troops the reason is to be found in the *red dragon*: "Although there are still more millions of spirits who are subordinate to those already mentioned, it is quite unnecessary to name them since they can serve a person only when it please the higher spirits to have them work."

We shall here name only the most important spirits of the infernal region whose powers in the province of sex are recognized by the most recondite authorities in their works on the Black Arts.

The great chiefs, the Emperor Lucifer, Beelzebub, and Prince Astaroth naturally represent the Almighty without being limited to any special duties. Under their command Satan as chief general has the delicate and enviable office of corrupting and seducing women and maidens. His special officers among the eighteen higher spirits are Pruslas, Aamon and Barbatos. Of the inferior spirits under him, we name only Sidragasum who has the power of "driving women sex-mad with dance."

What is the power of the demons?

The theologians are at one in recognizing them as very great and they explain this by the logical reason that although the demons were cast out of heaven, yet even in exile they kept their character as privileged beings and "forfeited none of the power of their divine nature as a result of the hierarchic order."

Tertullian ascribes the invention of the vain magic sciences, witchery and enchantment, to the love of women for the rebellious angels, and their later introduction into the most respectable arts of the toilette. "It is the rebellious angels," he declares, "who have made man acquainted with these worldly vanities. Legitimate work and industry have been corrupted into making the most foolish articles for the passions of vain women and have deprived mankind of its necessary sustenance. For no less did God, according to the witness of Henoch, damn the evil spirits to eternal darkness for having shown these dangerous materials to man, that is, gold and silver and the other works made of them, and the art of rouging the face and decorating the body."

§ 3

CULT OF THE DEMONS

ITS SACRILEGIOUS CEREMONIALS

What won so many hearts to Satan in the middle ages was the cruel and unpitying strictness of Catholic dogma in comparison to the completely human side of this secretive cult. For the Catholics, death signified the eternal separation except for the chosen few. For all others there was hell with its eternal torment. What comfort was afforded the troubled mother, the desperate widow, by this dreadful outlook for the beloved dead? Horrible punishment without the hope either for pity or pardon, a definite and absolute separation. To these troubled people, Satan, the king of the dead, gave new hope of seeing their dear ones again.

Michelet tells the story of a sorrowing widow who threw herself at the feet of an all-powerful sorceress and begged her for another sight of her beloved husband no matter what the cost even though it meant her life. The priestess of evil picked her up and said: "Turn back to your house; close your door well. Also close your windows on account of curious neighbors; put aside your mourning weeds and dress yourself in your bridal raiment; prepare his place at the table; but he will not as yet come; take from the closet the last garment that he wore and kiss it. Then you must say: 'The worst for you if you do not come.' Then drink down this bitter wine which will produce a deep slumber and you will sleep as a wife again. Be not doutful, now he will surely come."

Michelet relates further that the project was successful and that the husband promised to return every Sunday night provided that she was sleeping in bed at his arrival. He concluded: "This is a blessing that is not entirely without danger. What would have happened to the heedless woman if the church discovered that she was no longer a widow and that the spirit, awakened by love, had returned to comfort her?"

There was another cogent reason that led the people to the cult of Satan in the middle ages and at the beginning of the renaissance. The hypocrisy then underlying Catholicism was the unworthiness of its servants, who in spite of their oaths to be poor, modest and compassionate, were immodest and oppressed the poor, and thought only of collecting riches and honors. These factors combined in causing deep dissatisfaction among the people. While priests publicly preached castigation of the flesh, nocturnal orgies were celebrated in the palaces of the bishops, the homes of preachers, in convents and monasteries. Powerful persons could commit seduction and rape and the most disgusting unnatural debaucheries and go unpunished, provided that they paid large taxes or were otherwise in close harmony with the priests. Only the poor and the disinherited felt the harshness of religious laws. Oppressed by the tasks and impoverished by the tithes, the poor man had to suffer in silence as he saw the seducer of his wife and raper of his daughter blessed in church and his sins forgiven.

Hatred grew hot and began to boil among the people. Since God held his servants on earth accountable to him as co-workers and since the oppression continued unabated, they rose against God; but for this, as for every insurrection, a chief is necessary, a leader, who could fight on equal ground and weapons with the Eternal. Hence the people turned to the victim of the First War, Satan, the Prometheus of Christian mythology, the fallen archangel, in order to place him at the pinnacle again in a new battle. In fighting religion with religion, they called themselves the cult of the accursed and in the secret meetings held in the depths of the forest they proclaimed the Devil as their master. They performed the ironic and insulting ceremonies of the witches' sabbath and the Black Mass in contrast to the rites of despised Christianity.

The cult of Satan is thus also a religion and is indeed inspired by one of the Manichean heresies which, it will be recalled, taught of the eternal battle between the good and evil principles, between the god of light and god of darkness. "The cult of the demon is no more insane than that of God. One is corrupt and the other is resplendent, that is all. The affiliates of Satanism are mystics of a vile order, but they are mystics. It is high ly probable that their exaltation into the transcendentalism of evil coincides with the rages of their frenzied sense, for lechery is the wet-nurse of demonism."

Such is the idea that has led the worshipper of the devil to his choice. Refuge is found only in the good services of Satan, the procuration of physical joy denied either by lack of worldly possessions, physical disability, or some other insurmountable difficulty.

These reasons are the best explanation for the great number of priests who gave themselves up to Satanism in the Middle Ages. But to proceed logically, the only conclusion that can be drawn from these facts is that the first necessary and irremissable condition of being a complete worshipper of Satan consisted in a person being a fanatic Catholic, a devout believer in the wider significance of the world. Of what avail are these profanations of the host, these parodies of the mass to an Atheist or a Buddhist? What actual effect could they ascribe to the magic drinks or the maleficia brewed by the masters of the satanic art in a toxico-religious potpourri?

In this as in other branches of the secret mysteries, the initiates could always reply to the sceptics:

Nothing without Belief

A superfluity of religious practices affords the best temptations to occultism and the Eleusinian mysteries in their erotic aspects.

"From lofty mysticism to base Satanism is but one

step," explains Durtal in relation to the notorious Gilles de Rais. "In the beyond all things touch. He carried the zeal for prayer into the realm of *à rebours*. He was guided and controlled by that band of sacrilegious priests, transmuters of metals, and evokers of demons, by whom he was surrounded at Tiffauges.

"You think then that the Maid of Orleans was really responsible for his career of evil?" asked Durtal's companions.

"To a certain point. Consider. She roused an impetuous soul ready for anything, as well for orgies of saintliness as for ecstasies of crime."

We shall recount in the following chapters to what erotico-mystic perversions Satanism has led its devotees.

CHAPTER THREE

INCUBI AND SUCCUBI

§ 1

Demoniac Possession

THE CHALDEANS believed in the existence of sexless spirits who mingled with the moribund in their dreams, consumed their flesh and drank their blood. The Valkyrie of the Scandinavians, the Ephialte (nocturnal dwarfs) of the Greeks, the Dusii of the Gauls, all were connected with man. William Smith holds as a teaching of the Holy Bible that demons were actually present and effective in idolatry and that God permitted their evil designs up to certain degrees.

From this theory to the idea of possession is but one step: and it is very easily made. According to Ventura, the demon can seize the heart of an evil-doer; the demon transforms him into the object of his lusts, the satellite of his designs, the servant of his will. De Bonniot similarly states that the demon uses the heart of the miscreant as if it were his own property; but neither his entrance nor exit, nor even his presence in the body is physically felt. The possessed body is in a state of lifeless matter, a lost, masterless thing.

Or, as we define it, God, according to the theologians,

permits the pious to be exposed to the machinations of Satan up to a certain degree. Thus the blessed Angela de Foligno had to submit to the blows of demons who inspired her with evil wishes, but nevertheless did not succeed in transforming her desires into sinful passion. "His member is not yet in me," she said, "although I am beaten black and blue by demons, and have been laid low by his blows for many days and all my privates seem to be bursting."

§ 2

Copulations of the Incubi

Authentic Documents

Certain preliminaries are necessary in order to fully understand what constitutes *incubi* (male demons) and *succubi* (female demons). The gods and goddesses of ancient time knew how to transform themselves into incubi and succubi whenever they pleased. Jupiter made himself the incubus of Alkmene and Semele; Thetis was the succubus of Peleus, and Venus the succubus of Anchises. Satan also changed himself into an eagle or swan, a horse or bull, and even into a shower of gold.

Brognoli, who in his office as exorcist reported many cases of succubacy and incubacy, assures us that demons had the power of cleverly transforming themselves into an angel of light so that they could deceive and seduce women. But ordinarily, according to the demonologist, demons would assume the form of a small, dark and shaggy man with an enormous sexual member. His semen was cold and his embrace and coition were exceedingly painful.

Just as Jupiter would often change himself into a bull, so Satan possessed the power of assuming the form of certain animals. In a nunnery in the diocese of Cologne the convent dog was said to be a demon; the dog would lift the clothing of the nuns with his paw in order to copulate with them. Bodin, who reports this fact, nevertheless states that "it was no demon but a righteous dog." He adds however, that there was a woman in Toulouse of whom it was common gossip that her dog would violate her in this fashion even in public places.

In general, the women who were the victims of incubi had great distaste for their tyrants and considered themselves as stained beyond redemption.

A woman in Nantes had sexual intercourse with a demon who visited her every night while her husband was sleeping at her side and who noticed nothing unusual. After six long years of submission to the demon she confessed all to the priest, and the disgust provoked by this account caused her husband to leave her and left the incubus in sole possession of his victim. When St. Bernard one day came to Nantes, this woman begged him to free her from the demonic possession. The good saint told her to make the sign of the cross and to place in her bed at evening a stick which he gave her. When the incubus came that night to usurp the right of the husband, he found the stick of St. Bernard guarding the bed; all he could do was to fly into a passion with mighty threats; the barrier was insurmountable. A solemn ban pronounced by the Bishops of Nantes and Chartres in the cathedral completely freed this woman from the demonic possession.

Guilbert de Nogent relates that his mother had to defend herself against the attacks of an incubus on account of her great beauty. During a sleepless night there suddenly appeared to her "a demon whose custom it was to overpower those whose hearts had been torn by sadness," and who fell upon her and almost stifled her with his unbearable weight. The poor woman could neither move, cry out nor breathe; but she ardently prayed for divine intercession which luckily was not denied her. Her good angel appeared at the head of the bed and cried out softly: "Virgin Mary, help us!" and fell upon the incubus in order to force him to leave the room. The latter arose and sought to defend himself against the unexpected onslaught; but the angel threw him to the floor with such force that the entire house shook. The servants were aroused from their sleep and hastened to the bedchamber where they found their mistress pale and trembling. She recounted the danger which had threatened her, the clear marks of which she still bore.

Jean Bodin was present at the trial of a witch by the name of Jeanne Hervilliers, who was condemned in 1578 at Ribemont. This woman declared that she had been loved by a demon ever since her birth. At the age of twelve she had been deflowered by a demon who was invisible to all but herself. He did not leave her even after she married. In making this confession she added that the marital bed had been violated by this incubus for thirty years without her husband's knowledge.

The councillor De Lancre, who presided as royal commissioner over an inquisition on the epidemic of possessions that swept the country of Labourd (now the lower Pyrenees) in 1609, and who had more than eighty unfortunate women burnt at the stake in a space of less than four months, assures us that the devils possessed the means "of enchanting the women during the embraces of their husbands, and in forcibly breaking the holy bonds of matrimony they carried on adultery and lechery with them in the presence of their husbands, who became like immovable statues and were forced to watch their honor being violated before their very eyes without being able to prevent it. The woman, speechless, brought to silence by force, in vain implores her husband with her frenzied eyes to come to her aid; the enchanted man with folded arms and staring eyes must look on helplessly at his shame."

Authentic documents of this kind, that is, the decisions daily handed down during the trials of witches, present a woeful picture of the gallantry and generosity of the demons. To be sure the majority of the victims were so exceedingly unattractive that a man of taste can scarcely conceive what feeling could have forced the fallen archangel, the proud enemies of God, to stoop to such bizarre love affairs with ancient and withered crones.

Henriette Gillard, a rather ugly crone according to the executioner, confessed that she had the same intercourse with the demon "who took her to bed as wife, save that she found neither delight nor pleasure."

Nevertheless some women found pleasure in cohabiting with Satan. Johann Wier tells that in his time a fourteen year old nun by the name of Gertrude copulated every night with the august personage of Satan, himself. He caused her to be so enamored that she wrote the most passionate letters to him.

Madaleine de la Croix, abbess of Cordova, was considered a saint for a long time. Princes of the church, dukes, counts, savants, all the spiritual orders asked for her mediation. She finally confessed that she had been the paramour of the devil for over forty years, and that all the miracles she had wrought, to the great wonder of the populace, she owed only to Satan's aid. She related how she had concluded marriage with the demon and had given him two fingers of her hand as a mark of the contract and which had withered away since then. Even at the age of twelve she had caused miracles by this pact. The demon took on the form of a saint before whom she kneeled. She added that the demon who served her as incubus possessed the form of a handsome young man.

Jeanne Hervilliers of Verberie in Compiègne, confessed that her mother had presented her to the devil, who "took on the form of a great, black-horned and spurred man, also dressed in black, a dagger at his side, and a black horse before the door." Jeanne was twelve years old and since the day on which this presentation had taken place, the devil bedded carnally with her, like any man with a woman, except that his seed was very cold. This happened every eight or fourteen days. Jeanne was burned together with her mother.

De Lancre hence asserts that "the devil only rarely had sexual intercourse with maidens, since he could not commit adultery with them: he therefore waited until they were married."

The declarations made by the witches on the sensations during their infernal coitions, prove that the assumptions of Esquirol, Lamberg, Schrader, Rosshirt and others are incorrect: the witches were violated by men who assumed the masks of devils; on the other hand, they are very similar to the descriptions given by many female lunatics as to the face and form of the devil as seen in their hallucinations.

Cases have been known where women, after awakening from an anesthetic, declare they have been violated while under the influence of the drug. Nervous women also sometimes experience the venereal orgasm without any external causes. Moreover, the feeling of coition is a frequent symptom of certain nervous diseases, especially incipient spinal diseases.

Copulations of the Incubi

The hallucination of coition most frequently appears however in lunatics, and very often causes the formation of insane ideas and frequently rules the entire diseased organism. It is to be noted here that the diseased women are very rarely understood by their husbands and that coition is usually forced upon the unwilling woman, and hence associations of coition are extremely unpleasant. The entire sexual act becomes an evil mistreatment, over which the sick person bitterly complains. Descriptions of this kind by patients are very frequent, thus proving the impossibility of the occurrence. Thus, for example, an old woman bitterly complained that a certain physician would visit her every night and inject his penis into her ear penetrating down to her throat. Other patients believe themselves violated in similar, unnatural manners and complain about the violent pains caused by the forced coition.

These descriptions which the lunatics give of their hallucinatory copulations bear a close resemblance to the coitions with the devil.

That the intercourse with the demons was unpleasant and that their semen was cold was a well known fact, and was taught in the *Malleus Maleficarum, The Witches' Hammer*. It was confirmed by untold numbers of cases, and by the statements of the accused, sometimes forced from them by torture.

The witches also noticed during sexual intercourse with the devil that he had no back but was hollow like a kneading trough; that was already known by Cæsarius von Heisterbach. We read in the confession "with and without torment" of Anna Miller: "The devil had forced himself into her as often as he desired but he was hostile and of cold nature and his back was as hollow as a melter (a pitcher made of wood for milk or water)."

Other witches found intercourse with the devil to be still more unpleasant. At St. Claude in Jura in the last years of the sixteenth century Thiévenne Paget confessed that she had visited the witches' sabbath and that she had undergone sexual intercourse with the devil. His sexual organ was as long and as large as a finger; the coition was as painful as an ordinary confinement.

In the witches' prosecution which took place among the Basques at Labourd in 1609, many witches declared that the sexual favors of the devil were very painful, for his penis was as long as an arm and covered with fish-scales. Marie Marigrane, an accused girl of fifteen, asserted that the penis of the devil consisted half of flesh and half of iron; others explained that it was of horn. Some defendants related that coition with the devil was so painful that the women had to scream aloud as in the throes of child-birth. They were also drenched with blood after the sexual act.

These statements on the pain of coition with the devil coincide so remarkably with descriptions of the lunatics that we have just given, that it appears quite probable that the first account of infernal copulation was given by a female lunatic.

This theory is not disproved if later, when the peculiarities of the infernal embraces were made known to the witches' judges, the same accounts were given by women who underwent torture and did not suffer from hallucinations.

The *Malleus Maleficarum* contains a quotation in which can be plainly seen the hallucination of sexual intercourse without the unpleasant sensations usually found among the witches. It is asserted that a witch, nude to the navel, was found lying on the ground in an open field and making movements as if she were undergoing coition in pantomime. The devil was not visible to the spectators, although they declared that he was visible to the witch. This is either a case of hallucination or an hysteric fit, in which the above movements frequently take place.

§ 3

IMMORAL MYSTERIES OF THE SUCCUBUS

The succubus has always been a rarer phenomenon than the incubus. There are far more male than female devils. The reason for this perhaps lies in the fact that the power of the imagination of the man is less shameless and harder to pervert than that of the woman.

Balthasar Bekker notes that during the hundred and thirty years that Adam had intercourse with his wife, female devils came to him, became pregnant and bore devils, spirits, ghosts and phantoms.

Pico della Mirandola tells us that he knew an old man of eighty-four years who had slept for half of his life with a female devil; and another man of seventy, who had enjoyed the same advantages.

Sprenger reports that a German magician "had carnal connection with a woman before the very eyes of his wife and friends who were present during this action but were prevented from seeing her form."

Gregory de Tours tells of a holy bishop of Tuvergne, Eparchius, who had also been exposed to the temptations of a demon. He awoke one night with the thought of praying in the church; he arose and left for the church; on arriving he found the basilica resplendent with an infernal light and filled entirely with demons, who committed the most horrible deeds in front of the altar; he saw Satan in women's clothes sitting in the bishop's stool and presiding over these immoral mysteries. "Infamous whore," he cried, "thou art not satisfied with poisoning all and everything with thy pollutions, thou even defamest God's sacred spots with thy loathsome body."—"Since you give me the name of whore," answered the prince of demons, "I shall present you with many instances of it and will make you lust after the body of woman." Satan disappeared in a cloud of stench but he kept his word and poor Eparchius felt the torments of the fleshly appetites every night until his death.

The similar temptations of St. Anthony are too well

known to need repeating. Despite the saint's advanced and revered age Satan did not disdain from decorating his lonely hermitage with obscene and passionate pictures.

§ 4

INTERPRETATIONS OF THE INCUBUS

Dufour[1] states that the power of the imagination was alone to blame for all the nocturnal deeds that were ascribed to the demons. It was believed that darkness belonged to the infernal spirits, and that in the midst of the sleep of mankind the creator of sin and evil held full sway. Undoubtedly this arose from the belief in incubi and succubi.

In one of the last sittings of the Bureau d'Adresses, which was presided over by the physician, Théophraste Renaudot, the following problem was discussed: Can the devil propagate? One doctor had the presumption to assert that the incubi were only nightmares, "a hindrance of breathing, of voice and movement, connected with a pressing on the chest, which makes us believe in our sleep that a heavy weight is pressing on our breasts." Another speaker, also a physician, stated that "the incubus was not supernatural, but only a symptom of ani-

---

[1] Cf. *Recueil général des questions traitées et conférences du Bureau d'Adresses.* 5 vols., Paris, 1656.

mal faculty, accompanied by three circumstances: heavy breathing, hindered movement, and a passionate imagination." For him all this meant but a passionate imagination, "produite par l'abondance ou la qualité de la semence, laquelle, envoyant son espèce dans la phantaisie, elle se forme un objet agréable, remue la puissance motrice, et celle-ci la faculté expultrice des vaisseau spermatiques."

Alexander de Tralles similarly states that the incubus arises when the sleeper feels that he is suffocated and seems to be oppressed by demons. For Saint-André, physician to the king, it is at most "a chimera, which has no other cause than the dream, the sensitive power of imagination, and very frequently the imagination of women.... These have their share in the history of the incubus: a woman or a girl with a pretence to piousness is lecherous; in order to conceal their crimes they make out their lover to be an incubus who possesses them against their will.... It is the same with the succubus. Its source is to be found in the dream and in the sensitive imagination and often in the pinchings of the men. A man who has heard talk of the succubus, conjures up in his sleep the image of a beautiful woman who has intercourse with him."

These physicians showed a rare perspicuity and courage for their time and it is shameful that the pitiful figure of the parliamentary councillor De Lancre wielded so much power in the dark depths of his mind. The position of the judges was always that of a caste of narrow-minded and strait-laced spirits, and the officials of justice of the modern age are but little better than those of the Middle Ages, whose spirit and custom they have protected. It is they, who, in the midst of our modern civilization, are the true ghosts of the past.

CHAPTER FOUR

THE DEVIL'S COPULATIONS

§ 1

The Devil's Contract
Eleven Vilifying Ceremonials

THE DEVIL has two ways of copulating carnally with men or women: the one he uses with witches or magicians, and the other with men or women entirely removed from witchcraft. We have discussed the latter in the preceding chapter.

In the first case, the demon does not copulate with witches or magicians until after a solemn initiation as a result of which they yield themselves up to him. According to several authors who have reported the admissions of witches when on the rack, and whose recitals have been collected by Francis-Marie Guaccius in his *Compendium Maleficarum*, that initiation consists of eleven ceremonials:

First, novices have to conclude with the demon, or some other magician acting in the demon's place, an express compact by which, in the presence of witnesses, the novices enlist in the demon's service. In exchange the demon gives them his pledge for honors, riches and carnal pleasures.

Second, they abjure the Catholic faith, withdraw from

The Devil's Contract

their obedience to God, renounce Christ and the protection of the blessed Virgin Mary, and all the sacraments of the church.

Third, they cast away the crown, or rosary of the blessed Virgin Mary, the girdle of St. Francis, or that of St. Austin, or the scapular of the Carmelites, should they belong to one of these orders. Also the cross, the medals, the Agnus Dei, and whatever other consecrated object they have about their persons, they trample under foot.

Fourth, they vow obedience and subjection to the devil; they pay him homage and vassalage, laying their fingers on some cryptic black book. They bind themselves never to return to the faith of Christ, to observe none of the divine precepts, to do no good work, but to obey the demon alone and to attend diligently the nightly conventicles.

Fifth, they promise to strive with all their power and to give their utmost zeal and care for the enlistment of other males and females in the services of the demon.

Sixth, the devil administers to them a kind of sacrilegious baptism, and after abjuring their godfathers and godmothers, the baptism of Christ and confirmation, they are assigned a new godfather and a new godmother, who instruct them in the arts of witchcraft. They drop their former name and exchange it for another, more frequently a scurrilous nickname.

Seventh, they cut off a part of their own garments,

and tender it as a token of homage to the devil, who takes it away and keeps it.

Eighth, the devil draws on the ground a circle wherein stand the novices and witches, and there they confirm by oath all their aforesaid promises.

Ninth, they request the devil to strike them out of the book of Christ, and to inscribe them in his own. Then comes forth that cryptic black book on which, as has been said before, they laid hands when doing homage, and they are inscribed therein with the devil's claw.

Tenth, they promise the devil sacrifices and offerings at stated times: once a fortnight or at least each month, the murder of some child, or an homicidal act of sorcery, and other weekly misdeeds to the prejudice of mankind such as hailstorms, tempests, fires, cattle plagues, etc.

Eleventh, the demon imprints on them some mark, especially on those whose constancy he suspects. That mark moreover, is not always of the same shape or figure: sometimes it is the image of a hare, sometimes a toad's leg, sometimes a spider, a puppy, a dormouse. It is imprinted on the most hidden parts of the body: upon men, under the eyelids, or the armpits, or the lips, or the shoulder, the fundament, or elsewhere; upon women, it is usually on the breasts or the privy parts. The stamp which imprints these marks is none other than the devil's claw.

After the eleven ceremonials have been properly gone through, the novices promise never to worship the

The Spawn of the Devil

eucharist; to insult all saints and especially the blessed Virgin Mary, to trample under foot and vilify the holy images, the cross and the relics of saints; never to use the sacraments or sacramental ceremonials; never to make a full confession to the priest, but to keep always hidden from him their intercourse with the demon. The demon, in exchange, engages to give them always prompt assistance; to fulfill their desires in this world and to make them happy after their death.

Once the solemn initiation has been performed, each has assigned to himself or herself a devil called *magistellus* or assistant-master, with whom he or she retires in private for carnal satisfaction. The said devil is, of course, in the shape of a woman if the initiated person is a man; in the shape of a man, sometimes of a satyr, sometimes of a buck-goat, if it is a woman who has been initiated and who has thus become a witch.

§ 2

THE SPAWN OF THE DEVIL

ILLUSTRIOUS OFFSPRING

It is accepted by theologians and philosophers that carnal intercourse between mankind and the demon sometimes gives birth to human beings; that is how the Anti-Christ to to be born, according to some doctors, such as Bellarmin, Suarez, Maluenda, etc. They further observe that, from natural causes, the children thus begotten by incubi are tall, very hardy and bold, very proud and wicked. Thus writes Maluenda; as for the cause, he gives it from Vallesius, arch-physician in Reggio: "What incubi induce into wombs, is not just ordinary semen, but abundant, very thick, very warm, rich in spirits and free from serosity. This moreover is an easy thing for them, since they have but to choose ardent robust men, from whom they abstract an abundance of semen during copulation, and then women of a like constitution, also lying upon them, taking care that both shall enjoy the greatest delight possible, for the more semen emitted, the greater is the pleasure". Those are the words of Vallesius, confirmed by Maluenda who shows, from the testimony of various authors, mostly classical, that such associations gave birth to: Romulus and Remus, according to Livy and Plutarch; Servius-Tullius, the sixth king of Rome, according to Dionysius of Halicarnassus and Pliny the Elder; Plato the philosopher, according to Diogenes Laertius and Saint Hieronymus; Alexander the Great, according to Plutarch and Quintus-Curtius; Seleucus, king of Syria, according to Justinus and Appianus; Scipio Africanus the Elder, according to Livy; the emperor Cæsar Augustus; Messenian, an illustrious Greek commander, according to Strabo and Pausanias; also Merlin or Melchin the Englishman, born from an incubus and a nun, the daughter of Charlemagne; and, lastly, as shown by the writings of Cochlaus quoted by Maluenda, that damned Heresiarch ycleped Martin Luther.

§ 3

Magic Erotic Physiology of the Devil

"Sons of God with the Daughters of Men"

Giant Births

Before the flood, when the air was not yet so thick, demons came upon earth and had intercourse with women, thus procreating giants whose stature was nearly equal to that of the demons, their fathers. But now it is not so: the incubi demons who approach women are aqueous and of small stature; that is why they appear in the shape of little men, and, being aqueous they are most lecherous. Lust and damp go together; poets have depicted Venus as born of the sea, in order to show, as explained by mythologists, that lust takes its source in damp. When therefore, demons of short stature impregnate women nowadays, the children that are born are not giants, but men of ordinary size. It should, moreover, be known that when demons have carnal intercourse with women in their own natural body, without having recourse to any disguise or artifice, the women do not see them, or if they do, see but a barely perceptible shadow, as was the case with the female, who, when embraced by an incubus scarcely felt his touch. But, when they want to be seen by their mistresses, and to bring themselves to the delight of carnal congress, they assume a visible disguise and a palpable body. By what means this is effected is their secret, which our short-sighted philosophy is unable to discover. The only thing we know is that such disguise or body could not consist merely in concrete air, since this must take place through condensation, and therefore by the influence of cold; a body thus formed would feel icy, and so would not give pleasure to women in coition, but would give them pain; and it is the reverse that takes place.

The learned Father Sinistrari of the seventeenth century dissents in this opinion: The whole strength and efficiency of the human sperm reside in the spirits which evaporate and vanish as soon as issued from the genital vessels wherein they were warmly stored: all medical men agree on that point. It is consequently not possible that the demon should preserve in a state fit for generation the sperm he has received; for it is necessary that whatever vessel he endeavored to keep it in should be as warm as the human genital organs, the warmth of which is nowhere to be met with but in those organs themselves. Now, in a vessel where the warmth is not intrinsical but extraneous, the spirits get altered, and no generation can take place. There is this other objection, that generation is a vital act by which man, begetting from his own substance, carries the sperm through natural organs to the spot which is appropriate to generation. On the contrary, in this particular case, the introduction of sperm cannot be a vital act of the man who begets, since it is not carried into the womb by his agency; and, for the

The Devil's Copulations

same cause, it cannot be said that the man, whose sperm it was, has begotten the fœtus which proceeds from it. Nor can the incubus be deemed its father, since the sperm does not issue from his own substance. Consequently, a child would be born without a father, which is absurd. Third objection: when the father begets in the course of nature, there is a concurrence of two causalties: the one, material, for he provides the sperm which is the matter of generation; the other efficient, for his is the principal agent of generation, as philosophers agree in declaring. But in this case, the man who only provided the sperm would contribute but a mere material, without any action tending to generation; he could therefore not be regarded as the father of the child begotten under those circumstances; and this is opposed to the notion that the child begotten by an incubus is not his son, but the son of the man whose sperm the incubus has taken.

Besides, there is not a shadow of probability in what was written by Vallesius. Medical men are well aware that the size of the fœtus depends, not indeed on the quantity of the matter but on the quantity of virtue, that is to say of spirits held by sperm; there lies the whole secret of generation, as it is well observed by Michael Ettmuller: (Generation), says he, depends entirely upon the genital spirit contained within an envelope of thicker matter; that spermatic matter does not remain in the uterus, and has no share in the formation of the fœtus; it is but the genital spirit of the male, combined with the genital spirit of the female, that permeates the pores, or, less frequently, the tubes of the uterus, which it fecundates by that means. Of what moment can the quantity of sperm therefore be for the size of the fœtus? Besides, it is not always a fact that man thus begotten by incubi are remarkable for the huge proportions of their bodies. Alexander the Great, for instance, who is said to have been thus born, was very short. The poet said of him:

Magnus Alexander corpore parvus erat.

Besides, although it is generally a fact that those who are thus begotten excel other men, yet such superiority is not always shown by their vices, but sometimes by their virtues and even their morals. Scipio Africanus, for instance, Cæsar Augustus and Plato the philosopher, as is recorded of each of them respectively by Livy, Suetonius and Diogenes Laertius, had excellent morals. Therefore it may be inferred that, if other individuals begotten in the same way have been downright villains, it was not owing to their being born of an incubus, but to their having, of their own free will, chosen to be such.

We also read in the Old Testament, (Genesis, chap. 6, verse 4) that giants were born when the sons of God came in unto the daughters of men: that is the very letter of the sacred text. Now those giants were men of great stature says Baruch, (chap. 3, verse 26) and far superior to other men. Not only were they distinguished by their huge size, but also by their physical powers, their plundering habits and their tyranny. Through their criminal excesses the giants were the primary and principal cause of the Flood, according to Cornelius Lapide, in his *Commentary on Genesis*. Some contend that by sons of God are meant the sons of Seth, and by daughters of men, the daughters of Cain, because the former practiced piety, religion and every other virtue, while the descendants of Cain were quite the reverse; but, with all due deference to Chrysostom, Cyrillus, Hilarius and others who are of that opinion, it must be conceded that it clashes with the obvious meaning of the text. Scripture says, in fact, that of the conjunction of the above-mentioned were born men of huge bodily size: consequently, those giants were not previously in existence, and if their birth was the result of that conjunction, it cannot be ascribed to the intercourse of the sons of Seth with the daughters of Cain, who being themselves of ordinary stature, could but procreate children of ordinary stature; the reason is that it was not the common connection between man and woman, but the performance of incubi demons who, from their nature may very well be styled sons of God. Such is the opinion of the Platonist philosophers and of Francis Georges the Venetian; nor does it differ from that of Josephus the historian, Philo the Jew, S. Justinus the martyr, Clement of Alexandria, or Tertullian, who look upon incubi as corporeal angels who have allowed themselves to fall into the sin of lewdness with women. Indeed, as will be shown hereafter, though seemingly distinct, those two opinions are but one and the same.

If therefore these incubi, in conformity with general belief, have begotten giants by means of sperm taken from man, it is impossible, as aforesaid, that from that sperm should have been born any but men of approximately the same size as the one from whom it came; for it would be in vain for the demon, when acting the part of a succubus, to draw from man an unwonted quantity of prolific liquor in order to procreate therefrom children of higher stature; quantity has nothing to do here, since all depends, as we have said, upon the vitality of that liquor, not its quantity. We are therefore bound to infer that the giants are born of another sperm than man's, and that consequently, the incubus demon, for the purpose of generation, uses sperm which is not man's. But then, what is to be said?

Father Sinistrari, after thus excellently reasoning out the illogicality of the above opinions, offers his own theory, later supported by witch as by church:

"Subject to correction by our Holy Mother Church, and as a mere expression of opinion, I say that the incubus demon, when having intercourse with women, begets the human fœtus from his own sperm."

CHAPTER FIVE

THE WITCHES' SABBATH

§ 1

How the Witches' Sabbath Came About

Secret Assemblies

SATAN sometimes invited his devotees to the solemnities of his sabbath. According to P. Christian these assemblies were formed not only of wretches, beggars and bandits, but that high persons, masked and disguised, bribed their admission with gold. There the rich met the poor, the noble the low-born, the lady of the castle the inhabitant of the hut. Even the priests did not remain away and were given the title of "witch-priests."

The witches' sabbath was at most a contagious hallucination, an exceptional state of dreams, for which the magician prepared them by giving them certain drinks and intoxicating drugs to swallow. At any rate it is certain that secret assemblies in forests or caves formed the preludes of these visions and that there were concocted the sensual appetites according to spells and lechery which the intoxicating love-drinks did not fail to immediately realize in dreams comparable to that of the hashish- and opium-smoker. In order to be conveyed to the sabbath the person must rub himself with a salve, and swallow drinks sold by the magician; he must then pronounce certain magic phrases whose secret the initiates alone knew.

Bodin relates that a poor man who lived in the neighborhood of Loches in Touraine observed that his wife suddenly arose from her bed. She confessed to him that she was going to the sabbath and asked if he wished to join her. She smeared herself and her husband with a magic salve and the devil dispatched them into the vicinity of Bordeaux. The man became frightened, crossed himself, and invoked the name of God. Immediately everything disappeared, even the wife of this novice in witchcraft and he "found himself quite naked in an open field and wandered until morning finding the right path."

Bodin further tells a story of a "demoiselle" who had slept with her lover in Lyons. She rose very quietly from the bed, rubbed herself with salve and was borne away. Her lover who had seen everything, also rose and similarly rubbed himself, spoke the magic words and was also carried away. The sight of the devil and his horrible posture caused him remorse and he recommended his soul to God. Everything disappeared and our friend found himself naked in an open field. These same facts are repeated again and again in the *Capitularia regum*.

"It is notable," says Kiesewetter in his *History of Occultism*, "that the zealous opponents of the witches' trials such as Wier Spee and others gave a certain actual

How the Witches' Sabbath Came About

background to the witch, next to the polemics against the nonsensical beliefs of the devils and the horrors of the criminal procedure. This notable fact gives rise to the assumption that these men have not entirely risen above the superstition of their times." Injustice is done these worthy authorities with such assumptions for it must be said that in many aspects belief in witches rests on actual facts. Let us first see the flight of the witches to the sabbath.

Dr. Ludwig Meyer asserts that the entire witchery of the sabbath was due to an intoxicating drink, a decoction made from the thorn-apple and whose use called forth visions and dreams of devilish frolics. These aberrations in the minds of ignorant folks were held to be actual occurrences by the general public.

Meyer argues that all races have known intoxicating drinks and that from the earliest part of the Middle Ages old women knew how to prepare solanaceous poisons, the pleasure of which caused them to forget hunger and pain. And the time that the church formed the idea of the infernal societies, the gypsies had smuggled in the thorn-apple whose stimulating effect reinforced the belief in the incubus. The spreading of the witches is very closely connected with the broadening of the gypsy trail and the introduction of the thorn-apple.

This assumption of Dr. Meyer that the phenomena of witchcraft rests upon vision induced by narcotic methods is recognized as justified by Dr. J. L. Holzinger. But he is against the hypothesis that the thorn-apple was the narcotic employed, easily proving to his own satisfaction that is was as good as unknown in the previous century and was cultivated in gardens by only a few botanists.

§ 2

The Witches' Ride
The Witches' Aphrodisiac Salve

We shall now give a number of examples of the first kind of witches' ride whose frequent appearance in the sixteenth century led to the belief that the entire witchcraft was due to narcotics. The following story is told by Johann Nider:

A certain priest had declared that the witches' ride was untrue and was not physically carried out and that it was only product of the phantasy or dreams, and that the witches only imagined that they were carried to strange places and saw and heard things there which they related afterwards to others as gospel truth. An old hag with pretensions to magic took affront at this despisal of her magic art and at the close of services offered to prove to the priest that the witches' ride was no dream if he would accompany her home. The priest acceded. She then placed herself on a kneading trough on a bench and salved herself. She soon fell asleep and unconsciously moved about, threw her hands in the air, as if she would fly, was very restless, and sprang, as if

The Witches' Ride

she wanted to dance. She carried this on for some time, until she fell from the trough on to the ground. After she had lain on the ground for some time she moved, awakened, and cried out: "Now you have actually seen me fly away and return." "Indeed," said the priest, "you never flew away! You were lying asleep all the time in the trough until you fell to the ground where you have lain for some time until you just now awoke. Feel the upper part of your eye and see the wound you caused when you fell to the ground!" Thus the old crone was cured of delusion and the priest left, his belief strengthened that the witches' ride was non-existent.

The next account belonging here is due to the well-known magister of the papal palace, Dr. Bartholomew de Spina, who wrote his famous *Quæstio de Strigibus* in 1525. He says:

"The first to be mentioned is the occurrence of Prince N. and of which there are still eye-witnesses. In one of the local inquisitions a witch was imprisoned who declared that she had often been on the witches' ride. The prince desired to ascertain whether this was the truth or if it were purely imagination. He called the inquisitor and asked him to permit the witch to rub herself with the usual salve in the courtyard so that they might see whether it was an invisible or visible devil who carried her aloft in the air. When the inquisitor granted his request, she boasted that she would fly away from the courtyard as soon as she rubbed herself with the salve. She salved herself thoroughly but remained standing motionless, without anything out of the ordinary occurring. Therefrom it was deduced that the assumption of a physical ride was false and that it was but a deception of the devil if she believed it to be so.

"To reinforce this I would like to cite more examples that happened during my time. Augustus de Turre, a very famous doctor of our time, told me at his house at Bergamo that many years ago when he was studying at Padua he had returned home late at night and found no answer to his repeated knockings. He climbed in through the window of the first story intending to scold his servant, but found her senseless and lying entirely naked on the floor as if she were dead. He attempted to awaken her but all his efforts were in vain. He saw her the next morning when she had recovered her senses and questioned her as to what she had been doing the previous night. She confessed that she had been on the witches' ride. This shows clearly that those persons who believe that witches physically ride through the air deceive themselves, since it only happens to the spirit or in dreams while the person lies motionless at home.

"This is similar to the account given me by Dr. Petrus Cella, the vicar of the Marchese de Saluzzo, who told me that he had surprised his servant in a similar position and that she had confessed the same. The report also came to us that in the diocese of Como in the city of Lugano, the wife of a notary had been imprisoned by the inquisition there on charges that she was a night-rider and a witch.

The Witches' Ride

"Her husband who had held her to be a saint became suspicious in the following manner: One Good Friday he was unable to find his wife at home. He went to the pigsty and there found her lying naked with exposed genitals, completely senseless, and covered with the filth of the swine. Enraged and convinced of her guilt, he seized his sword and wanted to kill her. But he managed to compose himself and decided to wait for the end. In a short time she awakened and seeing that he wanted to kill her she fell at his feet and confessed that she had been on the witches' ride. When her husband heard this, he immediately reported her to the inquisitor, so that she would be burnt at the stake. But when she was sought, it was discovered that she had thrown herself into the sea rather than face public disgrace."

A similar and interesting observation in relation to the stimulating effect of the witches' salve was made by the physician of Pope Julius III., Andreas de Laguna (1499-1560). While treating the Duke of Guisa in 1545, a man and woman who lived in a hermitage in the neighborhood of Nantes were seized as magicians. A tub full of green salve was found among their possesions. Laguna analyzed it and found is was composed of extracts of hemlock salanum (nightshade), mandragora, henbane, and other narcotic plants. Since the wife of the local executioner was suffering from frenzy and insomnia he had her rubbed with this green salve. She slept for thirty-six hours and would have continued sleeping for a much longer period if she had not been aroused by very drastic measures, cupping-glasses among them. She complained bitterly at awakening for she declared she had been torn away from the arms of a handsome young man.

Another example belonging here is due to Porta, who also made the first attempt at a physiological explanation of the witches' salve:

"So greatly have evil desires mastered many people, that they misuse the beneficent gifts of nature and combine them to form witches' salve, which although bound up with many superstitions, nevertheless has many natural and effective powers. I here append the list of contituents as I have found them to be from actual examination and from the accounts of those who prepared them. The fat of an unbaptised boy, if possible, is cooked in an iron pot and strained together with eleoselinum, aconite, poplar branches, and soot. Or in another fashion: sium, acormum, solanum, oil and bat's blood. The members are rubbed until they are red so that the salve will work more quickly in the body. In this manner they believe they ride in the moonlight to feasts, plays, dances and in company with young people. And so forceful is the power of the imagination that the part of the brain in which memory resides is full of the details there impressed, and because their nature is very gullible, they conceive the impressions so quickly that the spirits in the brain are changed, the more so since they think of nought else night and day.

"This occurs more easily if those who use the salve eat

only mangel-wurzel, roots, greens, chestnuts and similar raw foods. Since I still thought very seriously about the matter, uncertain as to what I should make of it, I became acquainted with an old woman of whom it was said that she would enter houses at night and drain the blood from the children lying in the cradle. When I seriously asked her about the salve she told me I would have the answer in a few minutes. At that she told me and my friends whom I had brought along as witnesses, to leave the room. We could see her from a crack in the door completely undress herself and violently rub in the salve over her body. The power of the salve caused her to fall to the floor immediately and she sank into a deep sleep. We thereupon opened the door and found the stupor in which she lay so strong that she did not apparently feel the heavy blows which we rained upon her. We left until the effect of the narcotic salve would work off. After she awakened she told us of the marvelous things she had accomplished, how she had flown over mountain and sea, etc. Nothing that we could say would have any effect on her and when we even showed her the blue marks on her flesh that she had received from our blows she became more stubborn than ever."

Even Nicholas Remigius agrees that the witches could, by means of the salve, fall into an "iron sleep" in which they believed that they rode through far lands and saw palaces, gardens, springs, etc. When the judge had one of these women rub the salve on her body, she could be seen in violent movement on a stool, as if riding and spurring on a horse. Upon awakening the usual accounts of the splendors and miracles would be heard.

§ 3

BESTIAL CEREMONIES OF THE WITCHES' SABBATH

SATAN'S CHAMBER-POT

What happened in the evenings of the witches' sabbath? First, there was celebrated the Black Mass, the frivolous parody of Christianity, which we shall describe in the following chapter. After this blasphemous mass there followed a banquet in the open air, which was ended by a wild dance which led through the heat of the almost extinguished fire. From the complete darkness to the first onslaught of the sun, there took place scenes which even the boldness of a Petronius or a Juvenal would not dare describe.

Everything that the most bizarre and unnatural eroticism of abnormal minds could imagine took place there: practices of *stercoraires,* copromania, philotani, bestiality and pederasty.

Some writers have handed down to us various details of these ceremonies in which reminiscences of the ancient cults of Priapus and Pan are mingled in anomalous atavism with parodies of the Catholic divine services.

As soon as the participants have gathered in the designated clearing, the solemnities begin. The oldest one

Bestial Ceremonies of Their Sabbath

of the gathering, a wrinkled, sagging and rackety crone, takes care of the roll-call, then from out of a tub which she has brought there arises an indefinite shape which gets larger and larger. It is a colossal goat, a memory of the goat Mendes of the Egyptian mysteries. But it is here called "Master Leonhard" and is none other than Satan, himself. He receives the embraces of his true subjects who one by one kneel and kiss his buttocks. Then the youngest and most beautiful girl of the company is brought to him and is crowned Queen of the Sabbath. After a few preliminaries she is undressed and placed on an altar that has meanwhile been prepared. The subjects dip their left hand into a pit into which they have already urinated and make an inverted sign of the cross (parody of the sprinkling of the holy water). Satan then covers the altar and the victim with a kind of cloud and completes the bestial mystery of love; during the delay the company ape the example of their lord and master to the best of their abilities, not alone in couples but in groups of three and four! Suddenly the curtain of clouds is dissolved and all can see the "queen" lying outstretched on the altar while the devil is kneading dough on her buttocks, from which the infernal Host, the Host of the "Infernal Sins" is made. Sometimes the devil gives his subjects turnips or round pieces of worn out leather in place of the eucharist.

At the present time, say the authorities, the sabbath is celebrated only in outlying districts but the Black Mass still has many adherents, especially in the cities, since the magicians have left the country because of the easy discovery of their undertakings.

Let us make a thorough examination of the Black Mass and see what it really is.

CHAPTER SIX

THE BLACK MASS AND ITS ORGIES

§ 1

THE CULT OF THE MANICHEANS

BLACK MASS IN THE MIDDLE AGES

One of the most ancient religions, Manicheism, probably the simplest religion of all, had its peculiar customs, closely resembling a "Black Mass." It held that there were two principles, one of Good and one of Evil, a god of light and a god of darkness who fight for the souls of man. Psellus reveals in his erudite work *De operatione dæmonum* the fact that they tasted of the two excrements, urine and feces, at the beginning of their ceremonials, and that they mixed semen with the host.

Later, in the Middle Ages, came the Black Mass. It was, according to Michelet, a kind of salvation of Eve, who had been damned by Christianity. On the sabbath, just as in the Black Mass, the woman did all the tasks. She was the **priest, altar, host,** whom all the people enjoyed during their communion. The priest stepped on woman; he disapproved of all pleasurable intercourse with her, he damned her to eternal tortures which her unappeased sexual organs caused her, and let pass no opportunity of threatening her every act with the eternal guilt of Eve. Satan, on the other part, took the woman by the hand, picked her up from her degradation, glorified her, kissed her wounds, and they enjoyed together the blood of his eternal wounds, while he, for his part, trampled on the Christus created by the hated monks and priests.

The Black Mass is thus nothing more than a rendezvous of lecherous beings, who are there enticed by hopes of an erotic spectacle and a massive concluding orgy. It is the protest of the subjected people, the symbol of the longed-for freedom, the communion of rebellion. The woman who served as an altar was no longer an ordinary nymphomaniac, drunk with unknown passion, but became a true prophetess who risked both death and torture to cast off her bonds of despair, to hope for better times, and to attain the Host of love. There gathered the lovers, forcibly separated by the baron of the manor, and the poverty stricken people to complain on the one hand of the lost virginity of the maiden by the arrogation of the "first night privileges" of the baron, and on the other hand, of the impoverishing tithes of the church.

This conception of the Black Mass deprives it neither of its originality nor of its reality. To be sure it later took on an entirely different character.

§ 2

TRIUMPH OF THE BLACK MASS

IN THE

CENTURY OF LOUIS XIV.

MAGICAL APHRODISIAC PILLS

It was especially that resplendent century, the century of Louis XIV., which saw the triumph of the Black Mass. Dr. Légué in his work *Médecins et Empoisonneurs* presents a panorama of the ladies of the court of the great king passing in the little rue de Beauregard, that lonely street in one of the hidden, outlying quarters of Paris. They were going to Voisin, that famous female poisoner and magician. "All, yes all," he says, "wanted magic drinks to hasten the death of their hated husbands, or to enchant their lovers, to lengthen the vigor of a youth which debauchery had caused to dry up, to kill an unwanted embryo, fruit of a secret rendezvous, so that they might continue on the following day an excursion into the passionate field of sex.

"There were to be seen the most stout-hearted and dauntless women seized by an involuntary terror at the minute glow of a flickering lamp, while they read their fate in the coffee-grounds, in cards, in the damp entrails of freshly cut animals, in the magic mirror, and on the blackboard."

The author describes the arrival of Montespan in the

secret recess of Voisin's house. In one of the rooms there was erected a kind of altar, an anomalous altar, whose place was formed by a seat resting on a stand. The proud marquise did not shrink from completely undressing herself and placing her naked body upon the altar, so that on one side her legs hung free and on the other her head rested upon a pillow, supported by an inverted chair. The notorious Abbé Guibourg placed the cross between the breasts of the marquise, spread a napkin on her stomach, placed the communion cup there, and began the godless ceremony, in which Marguerite Voisin assumed the office of the priest. In the different phases of the mass, in which the celebrant must kiss the altar, the Abbé Guibourg kissed the genital parts of the Marquise de Montespan.

Why did the proud and haughty Atheneas, whom contemporary records describe as arrogant and aristocratic, stoop to such a horrible rôle and obediently allow herself to be the object of the slobbering kisses of the seventy-year old lascivious priest on her most private parts? Why did this so sensitive woman who would have shrunk at the slightest contact with the loathsome bourgeoisie, allow the murder of an innocent victim in the name of Satan? for this horrible priest cut the neck of a newly born child purchased from some poor and unfortunate woman, and let its blood run into the communion cup so that it could be mixed with the host and bring the favors of the damned to the participants! Why? The formula which the officiant spoke during the completion of the infernal sacrifice, informs us:

"Je (here follow the name, surnames and titles of De Montespan) demande l'amité du Roy et de Monseigneur le Dauphin et qu'elle me soit continuée; que la Reine soit stérile, que le Roy quitte son lit et sa table pour moy et mes parents; que mes serviteurs et domestiques lui soient agréables, que cette amitié redoublant plus que par le passeé, le Roy quitte et ne regarde Fontanges et que la Reine étant repudiée, je puisse épouser le Roy."

The apparent success of the Marquise de Montespan gave, as can easily be imagined, immense fame to Voisin, for she was naturally very discreet only as to those details which would be injurious to her. The Abbé Guibourg made a specialty of these abominations. He celebrated many masses on the abdomens of famous women, including Mme. d'Argenson and Mme. de Saint-Pont. The ritual of these ceremonies became standardized. Generally a child was kidnapped and burnt in a furnace out in the country somewhere, the ashes were saved and mixed with the blood of another child whose throat had been cut, and of this mixture a paste was made resembling that of the Manicheans. Abbé Guibourg officiated, consecrated the host, cut it into little pieces and mixed it with this mixture of blood and ashes. That was the material of the sacrament.

The good abbé also varied the proceedings, which undoubtedly had become monotonous to him, with *la messe du sperme*, a spermatic mass.

Guibourg, wearing the alb, the stole, and the maniple,

celebrated this mass with the sole object of making pastes for conjuring. The archives of the Bastille inform us that he acted thus at the request of a lady named Des Oeillettes: "This woman who was indisposed gave some of her blood; the man who accompanied her stood patiently beside the bed where the scene took place, and Guibourg gathered up some of his semen into the chalice, then added powdered blood and some flour, and after some sacrilegious ceremonies the Des Oeillettes woman departed bearing the paste."

In the eighteenth century there were many abbés who defiled holy objects. One Canon Duer occupied himself specially with black magic and the evocation of the devil. He was finally executed as a sorcerer in 1718. There was another who believed in the incarnation of the Holy Ghost as the Paraclete, and who, in Lombardy, which he stirred up to a feverish pitch of excitement, ordained twelve apostles and twelve apostolines to preach his gospel. This man, Abbé Beccarelli, like all other priests of his ilk, abused both sexes, and he said mass without confessing himself of his lecheries. As his cult grew he began to celebrate travestied offices in which he distributed to his congregation aphrodisiac pills presenting this peculiarity; that after having swallowed them the men believed themselves changed into women and the women into men. The receipt for these hippomanes is unfortunately lost. Beccarelli met with a very miserable end. He was prosecuted for sacrilege and sentenced in 1708 to row in the galleys for seven years.

A priest, Benedictus, cohabited with the she-devil, Armellina, and consecrated the hosts holding them upside down. Some priests even went so far as to celebrate the mass with great hosts which they cut through the middle and afterwards glued to a parchment, similarly cloven and used abominably to satisfy their passions. In other words, they practiced a most queer kind of sodomy, a Sacred Sodomy!

§ 3

Modern Societies

for the

Celebration of Satanism

Re-Theurgistes Optimates

As we have already mentioned, the ceremonies of the Black Mass are even performed in modern times.

The revue, *La Voix de la Septaine,* dated 1843, informs us that for twenty-five years, at Agen, a Satanic association regularly celebrated black masses, and committed murders, and polluted three thousand, three hundred and twenty hosts! In 1885 there existed at Paris and association composed of women, for the most part. These women took communion several times a day and retained the sacred wafer in their mouths to be spat out later and trodden underfoot or soiled by disgusting contacts. Even in the twelfth century there are numerous mentions of similar attempts at black masses in the daily journals.

Late in the nineteenth century the case of Cantianille turned not only the city of Auxerre, but the whole diocese of Sens, upside down. This Cantianille, placed in a convent of Mont-Saint-Sulpice, was violated when she was rarely fifteen years old, by a priest who dedicated her to the devil. This priest had himself been corrupted in early childhood by an ecclesiastic belonging to a sect of possessed which was created the very day Louis XVI. was guillotined. What happened in this convent, where many nuns, evidently mad with hysteria, were associated in erotic devilry and sacrilegious rages with Cantianille, reads for all the world like the procedure in the trials of wizards of long ago.

We have on the authority of a French savant that there are numerous societies throughout the world that celebrate Satanism and which are highly organized. "It is highly centralized and very capably administered. There are committees, a sort of curia, which rules America and Europe like the curia of a pope.

"The biggest of these societies founded as long ago as 1855 is the society of the Re-Theurgistes Optimates. Beneath an apparent unity it is divided into two camps, one aspiring to destroy the universe and reign over the ruins, the other thinking simply of imposing upon the world a demoniac cult of which it shall be high priest.

"This society has its seat in America. It was formerly directed by one Longfellow, an adventurer born in Scotland, who entitled himself "grand priest" of the New

Evocative Magism. For a long time it has had branches in France, Italy, Germany, Russia, Austria and even Turkey.

"It is at the present moment moribund, or perhaps quite dead, but another has just been created. The object of this one is to elect an anti-pope who will be the exterminating Anti-Christ. And those are only two of them. How many others are there, more or less important numerically, more or less secret, which, by common accord, at ten o'clock on the morning of the Feast of the Holy Sacrament, celebrate black masses at Paris, Rome, Bruges, Constantinople, Nantes, Lyons, and in Scotland, where sorcerers swarm!

§ 4

THE BEST AND MOST STRIKING ACCOUNT
OF
A BLACK MASS
THE SHUDDERING RITUALS

The best and most striking account of a Black Mass was given by Joris Karl Huysmans who presented it in the form of fiction, fearing that he would be laughed at if he told it as the gospel truth, although not only he, but many other prominent Parisians had actually been present during the ceremony We give the account in full as it contains all the customs and abuses of a typical Black Mass:

" 'This is the place'," said Mme. Chantelouve. She

rang. The grating opened. She raised her veil. A shaft of light struck her full in the face, the door opened noiselessly, and they penetrated into a garden.

" 'Good evening, Marie. In the chapel?' "

" 'Yes. Does madame wish me to guide her?' "

" 'No, thanks'."

"The woman with the lantern scrutinized Durtal. He perceived, beneath a hood, wisps of grey hair falling in disorder over a wrinkled old face, but she did not give him time to examine her and returned to a tent beside the wall serving her as a lodge.

"He followed Hyacinthe, who traversed the dark lanes, between rows of palms, to the entrance of a building. She opened the doors as if she were quite at home, and her heels clicked resolutely on the flagstones.

" 'Be careful'," she said, going through a vestibule.

" 'There are three steps'."

"They came out into a court and stopped before an old house. She rang. A little man advanced hiding his features, and greeted her in an affected sing-song voice. She passed, saluting him, and Durtal brushed a fly-blown face, the eyes liquid, gummy, the cheeks plastered with cosmetics, the lips painted.

" 'I have stumbled into a lair of sodomites. You didn't tell me that I was to be thrown into such company'," he said to Hyacinthe, overtaking her at the turning of a corridor lighted by a lamp.

" 'Did you expect to meet saints here?' "

"She shrugged her shoulders and opened a door. They

were in a chapel with a low ceiling crossed by beams gaudily painted with coal-tar pigment. The windows were hidden by great curtains. The walls were cracked and dingy. Durtal recoiled after a few steps. Gusts of humid, mouldy air and of that indescribable new-stove acridity mingled with an irritating odor of alkali, resin and burnt herbs. He was choking, his temples throbbing.

"He advanced groping, attempting to accustom his eyes to the half-darkness. The chapel was vaguely lighted by sanctuary lamps suspended from chandeliers of gilded bronze with pink glass pendants. Hyacinthe made him a sign to sit down, then she went over to a group of people sitting on divans in a dark corner. Rather vexed at being left here, away from the centre of activity, Durtal noticed that there were many women and few men present, but his efforts to discover their features were unavailing. As here and there a lamp swayed, he occasionally caught sight of a smooth-shaven, melancholy man. He observed that the women were not chattering to each other. Their conversation seemed awed and grave. Not a laugh, not a raised voice was heard, but an irresolute, furtive whispering, unaccompanied by gesture.

"'Hmm'," he said to himself. "'It doesn't look as if Satan made his faithful happy'."

"A choir boy clad in red, advanced to the end of the chapel and lighted a stand of candles. Then the altar became visible. It was an ordinary church altar; on a tabernacle above stood an infamous, derisive Christ. The head had been raised and the neck lengthened, and wrinkles painted in the cheeks transformed the grieving face to a bestial one twisted into a mean laugh. He was naked, and where the loin cloth should have been, there was a verile member projecting from a bush of horsehair. In front of the tabernacle the chalice, covered with a pall, was placed. The choir boy folded the altar cloth, wiggled his haunches, stood tiptoe on one foot and flipped his arms as if to fly away like a cherub, on pretext of reaching up to light the black tapers whose odor of tar and pitch was now added to the pestilential smell of the stuffy room.

"Durtal recognized beneath the red robe the 'fairy' who had guarded the chapel entrance, and he understood the rôle reserved for this man, whose sacrilegious nastiness was substituted for the purity of childhood acceptable to the church.

"Then another choir boy, more hideous yet, exhibited himself. Hollow-chested, racked by coughs, withered, made up with grease paint and vivid carmine, he hobbled about humming. He approached the tripods flanking the altar, stirred the smouldering incense pots and threw in leaves and chunks of resin.

"Durtal was beginning to feel uncomfortable when Hyacinthe rejoined him. She excused herself for having left him by himself so long, invited him to change his place and conducted him to a seat far in the rear, behind all the rows of chairs.

Celebration of a Black Mass

"'This is a real chapel, isn't it?'" he asked.

"'Yes, this house, this church, the garden that we crossed are the remains of an old Ursuline convent. For a long time this chapel was used to store hay. The house belonged to a livery-stable keeper, who sold it to that woman,'" and she pointed out a stout brunette of whom Durtal before had caught a fleeting glimpse.

"'Is she married?'"

"'No. She is a former nun who was debauched long ago by Docre.'"

"'Ah. And those gentlemen who seem to be hiding in the darkest places?'"

"'They are Satanists. There is one of them who was a professor in the School of Medicine. In his home he has an oratorium where he prays to a statue of Venus Astarte mounted on an altar.'"

"'No!'"

"'I mean it. He is getting old, and his demoniac orisons increased tenfold his forces, which he is using up with creatures of this sort,'" and with a gesture she indicated the choir boys.

"'You will guarantee the truth of this story?'"

"'You will find it narrated at great length in a religious journal, *Les annales de la sainteté*. And though his identity was made pretty patent in the article, the man did not dare prosecute the editors. What's the matter with you?'" she asked, looking at him closely.

"'I'm strangling. The odor from those incense burners is unbearable.'"

"'You will get used to it in a few seconds.'"

"'But what do they burn that smells like that?'"

"'Asphalt from the street, leaves of henbane, datura, dried nightshade, and myrrh. These are perfumes delightful to Satan, our master.'" She spoke in that changed guttural voice which had been hers at times when in bed with him. He looked her squarely in the face. She was pale, her lips pressed tight, her eyelids blinking rapidly.

"'Here he comes!'" she murmured suddenly, while women in front of them scurried about or knelt in front of the chairs.

"Preceded by the two choir boys the canon entered, wearing a scarlet bonnet from which two buffalo horns of red cloth protruded. Durtal examined him as he marched toward the altar. He was tall, but not well-built, his bulging chest being out of proportion to the rest of his body. His peeled forehead made one continuous line with his straight nose. The lips and cheeks bristled with that kind of hard, clumpy beard which old priests have who always shaved themselves. The features were round and insinuating, the eyes like apple pips, close together, phosphorescent. As a whole, his face was evil and sly, but energetic, and the hard fixed eyes were not the furtive shifty orbs that Durtal had imagined.

"The canon solemnly knelt before the altar, then mounted the steps and began to say mass. Durtal saw that he had nothing on beneath his sacrificial habit.

His black socks and his flesh bulging over the garters, high on his legs were plainly visible. The chasuble had the shape of an ordinary chasuble but was of the dark red color of dried blood and in the middle, in a triangle around which was an embroidered border of colchicum, savin, sorrel, and spurge, was the figure of a black billy-goat presenting his horns.

"Docre made the genuflexions the full or half-length inclinations specified by the ritual. The kneeling choir boys sang the Latin responses in a crystalline voice which trilled on the ultimate syllables of the words.

"'But it's a simple low mass,'" said Durtal to Mme. Chantelouve.

"She shook her head. Indeed, at that moment the choir boys passed behind the altar and one of them brought back copper chafing-dishes and inhaled deeply, then, fainting, unlaced themselves, heaving raucous sighs.

"The sacrifice ceased. The priest descended the steps backward, knelt on the last one, and in a sharp, trepidant voice cried:

"'Master of Slanders, Dispenser of the benefits of crime, Administrator of sumptuous sins and great vices, Satan, thee we adore, reasonable God, just God!

"'Super-admirable legate of false trances, thou receivest our beseeching tears; thou savest the honor of families by aborting wombs impregnated in the forgetfulness of the good orgasm; thou dost suggest to the mother the hastening of untimely birth, and thine obstetrics spares the still-born children the anguish of maturity, the contamination of original sin.

"'Mainstay of the despairing poor, Cordial of the Vanquished, it is thou who endowest them with hypocrisy, ingratitude, and stiff-neckedness, that they may defend themselves against the children of God, the Rich.

"'Suzerain of Resentment, Accountant of Humiliations, Treasurer of old Hatreds, thou alone dost fertilize the brain of man whom injustice has crushed; thou breathest into him the idea of meditated vengeance, sure misdeeds; thou incitest him to murder; thou givest him the abundant joy of accomplished reprisals and permittest him to taste the intoxicating draught of the tears of which he is the cause.

"'Hope of Virility, Anguish of the Empty Womb, thou dost not demand the bootless offering of chaste loins, thou dost not sing the praises of Lenten follies; thou alone receivest the carnal supplications and petitions of poor and avaricious families. Thou determinest the mother to sell her daughter, to give her soul; thou aidest sterile and reprobate loves; Guardian of strident Neuroses, Leaden Tower of Hysteria, bloody Vase of Rape!

"'Master, thy faithful servants, on their knees, implore thee and supplicate thee to satisfy them when they wish the torture of all those who love them and aid them; they supplicate thee to assure them the joy of delectable misdeeds unknown to justice, spells whose unknown origin baffles the reason of man; they ask, finally, glory,

Celebration of the Black Mass 91

riches, power of thee, King of the Disinherited, Son who art to overthrow the inexorable father!'"

"Then Docre rose, and erect, with arms outstretched, vociferated in a ringing voice of hate:

"'And thou, thou whom, in my quality of priest, I force, whether thou wilt or no, to descend into this host, to incarnate thyself in this bread, Jesus, Artisan of Hoaxes, Bandit of Homage, Robber of Affection, hear! Since the day when thou didst issue from the complaisant bowels of a Virgin, thou hast failed all thine engagements, belied all thy promises. Centuries have wept, awaiting thee, fugitive God, mute God! Thou wast to redeem man and thou hast not, thou wast to appear in thy glory, and thou sleepest. Go lie, say to the wretch who appeals to thee, "Hope, be patient, suffer; the hospital of souls will receive thee; the angels will assist thee; Heaven opens to thee." Impostor! thou knowest well that the angels disgusted at thine inertness, abandon thee! Thou wast to be the Interpreter of our plaints, the chamberlain of our tears; thou wast to convey them to the Father and thou hast not done so, for this intercession would disturb thine eternal sleep of happy satiety.

"'Thou hast forgotten the poverty thou didst preach, enamoured vassal of Banks! Thou hast seen the weak crushed beneath the press of profit; thou hast heard the death rattle of the timid, paralyzed by famine, of women disembowelled for a bit of bread, thou hast caused the Chancery of thy Simoniacs, thy commercial representatives, thy popes, to answer by dilatory excuses and evasive promises, sacristy Shyster, huckster of God!

"'Master, whose inconceivable ferocity engenders life and inflicts it on the innocent whom thou darest damn— in the name of what original sin?—whom thou darest punish—by the virtue of what covenants?—we would have thee confess thine impudent cheats, thine inexpiable crimes! We would drive deeper the nails into thy hands, press down the crown of thorns upon thy brow, bring blood and water from the dry wounds of thy sides.

"'And that we can and will do by violating the quietude of thy body, Profaner of ample vices, Abstractor of stupid purities, cursed Nazarene, do-nothing King, coward God!

"'Amen,'" trilled the soprano voices of the choir boys.

"Durtal listened in amazement to this torrent of blasphemies and insults. The foulness of the priest stupefied him. A silence succeeded the litany. The chapel was foggy with the smoke of the censers. The women, hitherto taciturn, flustered now, as remounting the altar, the canon came toward them and blessed them with his left hand in a sweeping gesture. And suddenly the choir boys tinkled the prayer bells.

"It was a signal. The women fell to the carpet and writhed. One of them seemed to be worked by a spring. She threw herself prone and waved her legs in the air. Another, suddenly struck by a hideous strabism, clucked, then became tongue-tied, stood with her mouth open, the tongue turned back, the tip cleaving to the palate. Another, inflated, livid, her pupils dilated, lolled her head back over her shoulders, then jerked it brusquely erect and belabored herself, tearing her breast with her nails. Another, sprawling on her back, undid her skirts, drew forth a rag, enormous, meteorized; then, her face twisted into a horrible grimace, and her tongue, which she could not control, stuck out, bitten at the edges, harrowed by red teeth from a bloody mouth.

"Suddenly Durtal rose, and now he heard and saw Docre distinctly.

"Docre contemplated the Christ surmounting the tabernacle, and with arms spread wide apart he spewed forth frightful insults, and at the end of his forces, muttered the billingsgate of a drunken cabman. One of the choir boys knelt before him with his back toward the altar. A shudder ran through the priest's spine. In a solemn but jerky voice he said, *'Hoc est enim corpus meum,'* then, instead of kneeling, after the consecration, before the precious Body, he faced the congregation, and appeared rigid, haggard, dripping with sweat. He staggered between the two choir boys, who, raising the chasuble, displayed his naked belly. Docre made a few passes and the host sailed, tainted and soiled, over the steps.

"Durtal felt himself shudder. A whirlwind of hysteria shook the room. While the choir boys sprinkled holy water on the pontiff's nakedness, women rushed upon the Eucharist and, grovelling in front of the altar, clawed from the bread, humid particles and drank and ate divine ordure.

"Another woman, curled up over a crucifix, emitted a rending laugh, then cried to Docre, 'Father, father!' A crone tore her hair, leapt, whirled around and around as on a pivot and fell over beside a young girl who, huddled to the wall, was writhing in convulsions, frothing at the mouth, weeping, and spitting out frightful blasphemies. And Durtal, terrified, saw through the fog the the red horns of Docre, who, seated now, frothing with rage, was chewing up sacramental wafers, taking them out of his mouth, wiping himself with them and distributing them to the women, who ground them underfoot, howling, or fell over each other struggling to get hold of them and violate them.

"The place was simply a madhouse, a monstrous pandemonium of prostitutes and maniacs. Now, while the choir boys gave themselves to the men, and while the woman who owned the chapel mounted the altar, caught hold of the phallus of the Christ with one hand and with the other held a chalice between 'His' naked legs, a little girl who hitherto had not budged, suddenly bent forward and howled like a dog. Overcome with disgust, nearly asphixiated, Durtal wanted to flee. He looked for Hyacinthe. She was no longer at his side. He finally caught sight of her close to the canon and, stepping over the writhing bodies on the floor, he went to her. With quivering nostrils she was inhaling the effluvia of the perfumes and of the couples.

"'The sabbatic odor!'" she said to him between clenched teeth, in a strangled voice.

"'Here, let's get out of this!'"

"She seemed to wake, hesitated a moment, then without answering she followed him. He elbowed his way through the crowd, jostling women whose protruding teeth were ready to bite. He pushed Mme. Chantelouve to the door, crossed the court, traversed the vestibule, and finding the portress lodge empty, he drew the cord and found himself in the street.

"There he stopped and drew the fresh air deep into his lungs."

CHAPTER SEVEN

WEREWOLVES AND VAMPIRES

§ 1

Werewolves

Lycanthropy for Sexual Sin

It is well known that witches can, at will, change themselves into werewolves or metamorphose human beings into similar beasts if they so desire. We need but refer to the familiar examples of the Greek and Roman deities which gave birth to a long list of followers in fact and fiction.

Many of the legends have been so changed by time, that it is only with difficulty that one is able to trace the real origin of the tale.

The familiar picture of Romulus, founder of Rome, suckling at the teats of a very respectable looking wolf, is a prominent example which can be duplicated even in the fairy tales of children by the familiar tale of "Little Red Riding Hood".

But the beginnings of lycanthropy, its mythological name, were far more serious and ominous. Baleful witches would turn themselves into the most ferocious beasts. The witches would also delight in inflicting the wolf's fever on some person who had aroused their ire

Lycanthropy for Sexual Sin 97

or who had not given in to their will. The victim would revert to the animal state, rip off his clothing, sulk in the forest and live as his prototype, the wolf.

This fearful scourge so impressed the ignorant people that it was looked upon as the greatest plight that could befall them. Indeed its effect was so great that it has come into our language expressing hopelessness: "The wolf is knocking at our door!"

The belief in lycanthropy is most prevalent in Hungary. If a woman commits any sort of a sexual sin she is immediately punished by being turned into a wolf. As late as 1867 the buxom wife of a Hungarian saddler who had given her favors to the beaus of the village locked herself in her house one night to escape the jealous onslaughts of the good housewives. When they broke in they saw a pile of feminine clothing in the center of the room and at the same time heard a cry of a wolf from a nearby wood. The assembled women hastily crossed themselves, but it was too late. For weeks the children of the district disappeared: their poor mangled bodies, pale and bloodless, being later found in the forest. The guilty wolf was finally caught by a band of men, exorcised by the priest, burnt at the stake, buried at the cross-roads and the pestilence ceased.

Belief in werewolves has lasted at least two thousand years and for a much longer time if it is identified, as it logically should be, with the teachings of animism, according to which the soul of a man leaves his body at death and enters the animal kingdom, assuming the body of some beast or bird.

And that belief in lycanthropy exists today, the daily newspapers bear witness. Scarcely a month goes by in which a "good" wolf story does not come from a Danubian country or a *loup-garou* from the Canadian wilds.

§ 2

Vampirism

We touch on the problem of belief in vampires but slightly, since it is closely related to incubacy and succubacy, of which it is certainly a derivative branch.

The dead who arise from their tombs in order to feed themselves on passion and blood, maidens enticed from their coffins by desire for earthly joys, returning in the dark to their beloved, living beings seized by an exercrable love and becoming corpses with pale lips and closed eyes; of such were the legendary heroes of vampirism of the entire Middle Ages.

The Bukovaks of the Bulgarians are but the Scythian vampires, the ghouls of the Arabians and the lamia of the Greeks.

A citation of Herodotus, wherein he speaks of embalmment, proves that even in Thebes and Memphis vampirism found many ardent believers in that society which

Vampirism

had the greatest respect for the dead. "As far as concerns the noble ladies," says the Greek historian, "their bodies were not immediately given to the embalmers, especially those who were of great beauty and who attracted great attention during their lifetime, but were given them three or four days after death. These precautions are taken because it is feared that the embalmers will violate the corpse. It is said that one of them was discovered *in flagrante delicto* with the body of a recently deceased maiden, and the complaining witness was indeed his colleague."

In our times the law courts record a good number of such necrophiliac cases, increased by the number of violators of graves. The active vampirism of living beings on the dead belongs more to the field of sexual perversions than to that of black magic.

Legendary vampirism, in which the dead are the malefactors themselves, is, as we have already said, closely related with incubacy.

The Greek, Arabic, Turkish and Roman legends are filled with tales of vampires. Among all these people, the vampire was an actual creature who had to be most firmly curbed.

All the stories of vampirism closely resemble one another. Wickwar retells a famous and actual account of a vampire who plagued Belgrade. The story goes that a young man named Arnod returned from Cossova where, he declared, the people were dying of fright on account of their friends being bitten by a vampire. He himself had not been bitten; but he had been in the vampire's presence, and the vampire had made him understand that he was soon to die and become a vampire also. Sure enough, a few days afterwards he fell into a death trance and was buried.

Three weeks afterwards a girl named Nina, who had known him, together with some neighbors, complained that a vampire was haunting them with unwelcome attention. and that four people had been bitten in the neck and had died in consequence.

Such a serious state of affairs could not be allowed to continue; so the authorities, on a grey morning a day or two afterwards, made up a nondescript party consisting of a sexton, two surgeons, armed with spades, pickaxes, and ropes, together with one drummer boy from the army carrying a lantern and a box of surgical instruments, and they wended their way to the churchyard where Arnod, the vampire, lay buried.

Their intention was to find out for certain whether he was a vampire or not. If he proved himself to be one, he would be treated as all vampires were treated.

They reached the cemetery, found the grave they were in search of, and began to dig with a right good will. Presently, the pickaxe struck the coffin lid and pulled it off, and there was Arnod lying on his side "asleep."

The sexton pulled him over, gazed at him, and then in a voice of triumph cried out, "What! Your mouth not wiped since last night's escapade!"—and other things eminently suitable to the occasion. At this the spectators shuddered; the boy dropped the lantern and the instruments into the grave and promptly fell in after them.

When the boy, the lantern, and the instruments had been picked up, sorted out and put together again, further attention was paid to Arnod.

As we expected, he proved himself a true vampire, for "his face did have a complexion upon it" and he "did appear as though he had not been dead a day." So without any further ado he was spiked and as this was being done "the corpse groaned." The body was then taken up, burned as if it were a witch, and the ashes scattered to the wind.

Other coffins in the same cemetery being opened, were found to contain vampires, so a similar treatment was meted out to them. Even such decisive measures as these, however, failed to extinguish the evil which was believed to be blighting the village, so a more severe method was inaugurated.

The authorities had all the graves opened, every body was anatomized, and where it was thought advisable, the bodies were treated as Arnod's had been.

These happenings, as improbable as they may appear to have been, are recorded as having taken place at Mednegna, near Belgrade, in 1832. The report is signed by three regimental surgeons, and countersigned by a lieutenant-colonel and a sub-lieutenant.

CHAPTER EIGHT

SEX ENCHANTMENTS

§ 1

Amatory Witchcraft

Ancient Love Enchantment

WITCHCRAFT has been practiced in all ages not only from motives of hatred but equally of love; the methods, however, of attaining these diametrically opposed purposes were almost always the same.

The ancient poets have saved for us the common invocations and the ordinary formulas in their love-poetry. Undoubtedly they have prettified, decorated and interwoven them in the pearls of their verse but they have at the same time retained for us the spirit and the intention as well as the entire ceremonial of the enchantments.

"I have fashioned two puppets," says the enchantress, "one of clay and one of wax."

"The clay hardens in the glow which thou kindlest, Amaryllis, the wax melts, and may our love cling together in the rising flames."

"May he be as cold as ice to those who tempt him, but weak as a babe in my enticing arms. O enchantress, one of clay and one of wax."

The tradition of these puppets of clay, wax and similar substances appears to be universal in enchantments of this kind for the invocation of love or hatred. It is to be met in the ancient times of the Assyrians, Egyptians, Greeks and Romans. It remained during the middle ages and is even to be found today in many savage races, among the Malays and the Polynesians in Borneo.

A recent number of the *Revue des Deux-Mondes* contains a description of an enchantress of Borneo, who was accused of destroying her rival, a young woman, by making a waxen picture of her and exposing it to the fire. Her rival was later found to be fatally burnt in the same places that the image had melted away.

Ibn-Khaldun, secretary to the King of Granada who lived in the fourteenth century, tells in his *Prolegomena* of the following surprising facts of which he had been an eye-witness: "We saw with our own eyes how one of these black magicians prepared the image of a person whom he wanted to enchant. The image consisted of materials prepared according to the orders of the magician and whose symbolic significance harmonized with the nature and position of his victim. After the magician had placed before him the image of the symbolized person, he muttered some words over it, spat on it, moved its members while pronouncing the letters of the dread, magic formula; finally he placed a cord about it, and tied a firm knot in it, thus signifying that he had performed his duty with firmness and steadfastness and had concluded the pact with the demon who had helped him at the moment of the ejection of the saliva, proving that he cherished the firm desire of making the magic inextricable. An evil spirit, hidden in the saliva of the magician, was thus implanted on the symbolic image and would call on the other evil spirits to aid him, thus enabling the magician to carry out whatever evil designs he might have against the person."

§ 2

WORKINGS OF MAGICAL OPERATIONS
CASE OF BISHOP GUICHARD   HIS CONFESSIONS
HIS MAGICAL METHODS OF CAUSING LOVE IN OTHERS

In the Middle Ages increasing use was made of enchantments, especially witchcraft, as vengeance for unrequited love.

A valuable document of this period enables us to observe the workings of this two-fold magical operation. It is the public report of the case of the Bishop of Troyes, Guichard, whom the public had named the *fils de l'incube*.

This lecherous bishop and magician, thirsting for riches, is one of the weirdest figures of the fourteenth century. Of doubtful origin, the devil was popularly supposed to have been his father; the young Guichard was brought up in a house where ghosts would come and go at all times as a matter of course — as he later revealed in his confessions. It may be asked how a young man with such prerequisites could honorably prepare himself for priesthood, and why he was destined to at-

Case of Bishop Guichard

tain the clerical rank. The answer probably lies in the fact that the monks and priests of that time were extremely powerful and that this career led rapidly to wealth, power and regard.

Guichard quickly reached the first honors. In a few years he had attained a bishopric and one of the wealthiest prebends of Champagne. Public opinion, indeed, did not refrain from saying that he had hastened the deaths of his predecessors by poison, but the young prelate was so keen a diplomat that these slanders formed no hindrance to his attaining the protection of his mighty mistress, Jeanne de Champagne, Queen of Navarre. Shortly thereafter she was married by Philip the Handsome and became Queen of France. With her aid Guichard attained the much envied position of councillor to the King.

Detestable actions, unscrupulous means in enriching himself, revolting misuse of the privileges of his office, rapidly brought the attention of his superiors to this new bishop. He could have faced them disdainfully if dissension had not broken out between him and the queen, — or more correctly, queens; for Jeanne's mother, the dowager Blanche, became frightened for her daughter's sake and did not rest until the king had dismissed him. By a strange coincidence both queens died at about the same time that an investigation was being held on the abuses of the accused bishop. Public opinion arose against Guichard and dreadful complaints of enchantments rang throughout the entire province.

That was the end. The bishop was seized and thrown into one of the towers of the Louvre as a prisoner of state.

Bishop Guichard was accused of causing the death of Jeanne of France by magic operations, after failing to win her love.

In spite of the denials of the defendant, many eyewitnesses of his crime sprang up, among them being a Jacobin hermit, and an enchantress, his aid, a "femme inspiritée."

The hermit, apparently no saint, declared that Guichard had come to his hermitage at Saint-Flavy and had there called an enchantress to aid him in making the queen enamoured of him. The specialist had then declared that she did not have the power of so doing, and that thereupon the enchantment of the queen was decided upon. So well were the rules of enchantment followed that she died as a result.

For her part the enchantress said to the judges that the bishop called her and asked whether she had the means of causing the queen to fall in love with him, whereupon she answered, "No." The bishop had then called the Jacobin and told him that she was powerless to help him; the Dominican friar answered that the magic books must be read and faithfully followed; the bishop followed his instructions and a devil immediately appeared on the spot; the Jacobin discussed with the devil on how the bishop could have his pleasure with the queen and that she had not heard his answer; that she, the witch, knew many infallible methods of causing love to appear between two persons but that she had been unwilling to tell them to the bishop...

We shall see what some of these means were and how efficacious they proved to be, in the following sections.

§ 3

Mystic Methods to Win the Love
of a
Man or a Woman

The common puppet was not always used as a means of enchantment in the Middle Ages. The *Archives de la Bastille* have provided us with the most powerful formulas of the secretive Brinvilliers:

"Throw a fagot with incense and alum into the fire and speak these words: Fagot, I burn thee, as the heart, the body, the blood, the understanding, the movement, and the spirit of X (man or woman). That he may not come to rest, nor may he remain in a spot, nor speak, ride, drink nor eat until he has done what I desire of him."

In a word, the invocation remains about the same: there is needed either a portrait or some other likeness, a fagot sufficing. To be sure the formula does not say much and we must assume that before the fagot has undergone the magic operation it must have somehow been treated so that the personality of the victim had been drawn to it.

Other and more mystic methods are:

To gain the love of a girl or woman, you must cast her horoscope and must make her look right into your eyes. When you are both in the same position you are to repeat the words, *"Kafe, kasitanon kafela et publia fillii omnibus suis."* These words said, you may command the female and she will do anything you like no matter how vile or obscene it may be.

Another way to gain the love of a person, be it male or female, is to rub your hands with the juice of vervain and touch the man or woman you wish to inspire with love.

Perhaps the simplest of all is the following, although we cannot guarantee results to the reader unless it so happens that his female companion has also read this work: While touching the girl's hand with your own you must say the following words: *"Bestarbetto corrumpit viscera ejus mulieris."*

§ 4

Enchantments by Means of Photographs

The advances of modern times have caused changes in the procedures of enchantments. No longer is it necessary to spend long hours on preparing a likeness or using fagots. A photograph of the pertinent victim suffices.

Moreover the theory of enchantment by means of photographs is certainly not new. Even Paracelsus had turned to it; have respect for its hoary age! This famous occultist, the father of black laws stated that a part of the sensitive properties of the subject were attracted to the picture and remained fixed there. According to Paracelsus sensitive persons whose pictures are maltreated suffer the same injuries on the corresponding parts of their bodies.

This theory has been adopted by many investigators, especially in France by Rochas and Lermina. The latter studied and analyzed in his novel, *l'Envoûteur*, the hypothesis originating with Balzac, that a person who allows himself to be photographed loses a part of his personality and aura which has been attracted to the sensitive film.

The black magicians of the nineteenth century knew this theory by intuition. The pretty ladies of the theatre, the favorite tenors of the operas, the literati, the artists, in short all those whose pictures fill the show-windows, have unconsciously been the effigiac objects of magic operations.

§ 5

Modern Magic Formulas

Love-Drinks   Flesh   Talismans   Love-Inks

Jules Bois divides the enchantments of love into three classes. The first relates to the customs of the Greeks and the Romans, as Theocritus and Virgil have handed down to us, employing wax pictures and verses. In the second class there are employed solid or liquid foods: fruits, flesh, different drinks. In the third class are used love-drinks, that is, in almost all ages: aphrodisiacs, herbs, and talismans.

We have already spoken of the first in some detail so we can here dispense with it almost entirely.

The second class is apparently far more potent. Among the means of nourishment, fruits are the most used, and among them the most popular is the apple. The apple, the object of sensual desire of our Mother Eve, "the Challenger of the Gourmand," is also excellently adapted to be an interpreter of love, it forms an excellent conductor, magnetically speaking.

Modern Magic Formulas

In the following passages the author of *Satanisme* introduces us to the erotic properties of this fruit, also to the art and method of its application.

"Clavicula teaches that in order to make this fruit unsurpassable, it must be perfumed and sprayed before being plucked. Thereupon one must say:

"O God, who created Adam and Eve out of the four elements, how Eve actually handed down evil to Adam and brought him to sin, so shall he who eats of this fruit carry out forever my desires."

If apples are lacking, other foods can be used if the following formula is spoken:

"In whatever part of the world ye find yourselves and with whatever names ye name yourselves, I invoke ye, O demons, who are possessed of the power of throwing the hearts and minds of men and women into confusion, come this night into this fruit and influence it so that it will also partake of the power of causing whatever man or woman I may so desire to be attracted irresistibly to me with love."

This strange benedicite undoubtedly served as a prelude to the orgies of the debauchees of the middle ages and many a seducer has chanted it after a consultation with the notorious Florentine Ruggieri, before he took refuge in that last desperate means of the magic art, the magic drinks, the amulets and the talismans.

We might also mention the more poetic use of sympathetic inks. These inks whose effects are held to be infallible and which are called love-inks, are compounded of the ashes of love letters, powdered magnetic stones and women's milk. To make absolutely certain of its success the love-ink must be used only on virgin parchment, of which the *Dictionnaire infernal* gives the detailed recipe. The parchment is prepared from the skin of a dead animal which had never engaged in coition. After it has passed the ritual operations, it is suitable for the sympathetic love-ink, although it must not be seen by any woman (with the natural exception of the receiver) in order for its full strength to be retained.

§ 6

Danger of Enchantments

It often happens that the enchanter by a kind of rebound becomes the enchanted one himself. "Let the one," says Bois, "who intends to have a passionate love break out in some person, take the greatest care, lest it result in his falling in love. In as much as the image of the person he wishes to possess goes so strongly to his own body, he places himself in the danger of becoming the possessed and not the possessor. The fire which he kindles may turn upon himself and penetrate into the depths of his heart."

§ 7

STRANGE CASE OF GAUFRIDI
SEDUCTION OF WOMEN BY HIS BREATH
PRINCE OF MAGICIANS BURNT IN PUBLIC

In earlier times these practices often had tragic results to those who tried to apply them. We limit ourselves in summary descriptions to two of these cases, each one a veritable drama: the case of Louis Gaufridi and the case of Urbain Grandier.

Louis Gaufridi, a priest of the church at Accoules at Marseilles, was considered to be a model of all the virtues until a strange occurrence caused his sudden imprisonment at the behest of the inquisition. Great consternation was caused in the city for Gaufridi had been as much loved as he was honored. What could occasion the appearance of such a holy man before this body of inquisitors? The alarm was general when it was discovered that he had been formally charged by the Ursulines at Aix with seduction of inmates, of handing them to the devil and of having been one of the most ardent adepts of Satanism. Public opinion rose in wrath against such a slander and it was felt that Gaufridi would soon be declared innocent. The defendant protested his innocence in front of his accusers, Madeleine de Mandol and Louis Capel; but later the abuses which the hysterical girls threw at him seemed to weigh him down, and he became confused and entangled in his answers. He was led back to his prison and two exorcists were called to bring him to speech.

Our criminal officers of today may have all the modern weapons of science to call upon in questioning suspects, but the inquisitors of the old days needed no fancy instruments to get the desired information. The victim resisted their questions for a time, but his gradually weakening state caused him to break down and confess all they wanted him to.

All the fanatic delusions of the inquisitors were necessary for them to fail to perceive that it was a madman who was telling them the most hair-raising stories.

Gaufridi related that at the age of fourteen years, while reading a book belonging to his uncle, Lucifer appeared to him and after concluding a solemn pact he was granted the power of seducing all women merely by his breath. More than a thousand women had been violated by him because of his irresistible breath. Among these was the mother of his accuser, the Madeleine de Mandol. The latter also had been breathed upon by him, although she might have been his own daughter for all he knew, and she was just as little able to resist him as were all the others. An insane passion had thrown her into his arms and she had given herself up to all debaucheries with him, partly in the orgies of the witches' sabbath, and partly in the quiet of the convent.

On the sabbath he had received from Satan himself the title of Prince of Magicians.

Gaufridi was condemned to be burnt in a public place. Those whom he had seduced led a most wretched life, continually hearing the taunts of the people and heavy breathing and snoring wherever they went.

§ 8

Case of Urbain Grandier

His Phenomenal Power over Women

Urbain Grandier was the handsome priest, the elegant confessor, the fiery preacher, over whom women become insane with love even at first glance. Educated, a favorite writer, provided with high spiritual honors by the protection of the Jesuits, the priest of Saint-Pierre de Loudun had the great fault of being very conscious of his personal value and never bowing himself before anyone, no matter whom. It is told that he had many quarrels over precedence with Richelieu, when the future alter ego of the thirteenth Louis was still but a simple priest in Coussai.

Gossip about the favors women extended to him filled the entire province. He did not deny it and even carried his boldness so far as to carry on a public love affair which led in a singular fashion to his downfall.

His fame carried over the walls of the Ursulines at

Loudun, especially since the post of confessor of these nuns was open and the priest of Saint-Pierre was the logical choice. But his enemies were many, and despite the pleas of the nuns the post was given another. Scarcely had the unfortunate rival of Grandier entered his office than the phenomenon of possession seized the nunnery. After due exorcism, the Ursulines abandoned his name to his enemies. He was accused of concluding a pact with the devil by which he was to hand over to his infernal majesty the hearts of the nuns. Such an accusation could become very dangerous. Grandier aggravated the danger by his haughty mannerisms.

The following were the bases of the accusations:

"It must not be forgotten," said the judge, "that all these nuns at the mere mention of the name of Grandier were seized with confusion and convulsions and at the confrontation, at which physicians were present to see what exceptionable excitement was caused, they became greatly inflamed, just as did the secular women who were seized with love for the defendant."

The testimony of the latter follows:

The first said that when the priest one evening looked straight into her eyes she was seized by a sudden and weighty love for him.

The second, that on casually meeting her in the street, he pressed her hand and that by this simple contact she became extremely passionate and madly in love with him.

The third, that on seeing him enter the church at

Carmes, she became suddenly restless and lusted after him.

In addition, eighteen nuns, eight of whom were possessed, and six women confessed that they had had a sinful love for the preacher of Saint-Pierre. Many of them had visions of him in their sleep.

In the face of such powerful evidence what else could the Inquisitors do but condemn him to death as an agent of the Devil?

§ 9

Erotic Fascination
Case of Castellan
A bold Public Exhibition of Physical Fascination

Many cases of love-enchantments of former times are clearly explained today in the light of our modern knowledge of suggestion, and especially that form of suggestion known as fascination. We understand that secret degree of mental influence upon a partly-awake person which causes him to become an obedient, willess toy of another individual, obeying his every command. We here tell of some of the more interesting cases of this nature.

The first is fully recorded in the assizes of Draguignan.

At the end of the nineteenth century a beggar, named Castellan, came to the village of Guiols. He was twenty-five years old and crippled in both legs. In this village there lived a certain Dourban, who had a sixteen-year old daughter with an unsullied reputation. Castellan turned to these people for hospitality, pretended to be a deaf-mute and made known by signs that he was hungry. Invited to eat with them he drew the attention of his host by his notable behavior; he did not allow his glass to be filled before he made the sign of the cross over it and over himself. In the evening he gave them to understand that he could write, and wrote the following sentences: "I am the Son of God; I come from Heaven and my name is: Lord Master. You see my little miracle and soon you will see my great miracle. Be not afraid, for God has sent me to you."

He also informed them that he could predict the future and prophesied that civil war would break out in six months. These insane statements made a great impression on all the spectators and in particular on Josephine Dourban; in fear of the beggar she slept in her clothes. The latter spent the night in a haystack and left the village the next morning after breakfast. After he had ascertained that Josephine would remain home alone the entire day, he returned. He found her busy at household tasks and conversed with her for a long time by symbols. He spent the whole afternoon there practicing a kind of fascination upon her. A witness testified that he saw her inclined over the hearth while Castellan drew circles on her back with his hand and made the sign of the cross; she then had a fixed and vacant stare. It is quite possible that he had then placed her in a somnambulistic state. At midday they both sat down to eat and scarcely had the meal begun when Castellan made a movement as if he were throwing something in her spoon. The maiden immediately became unconscious; Castellan picked her up, carried her to the bed, and there abused her sexually. Josephine understood what was being done to her, but an irresistible force prevented her from struggling or crying out. She was in the lucid stage of lethargy. Even after she came to, she remained under the power of the man and when he left the village in the afternoon, she was driven by an irresistible power to follow the beggar, like a senseless wild animal, although she had the greatest dislike and horror for him. They spent the night in a haystack and the next morning walked to Collobrières. A certain Sauteron met them on the way and invited them to stop with him. Castellan told him that he had seduced the maiden. Josephine also complained to him of her despair and added that she wanted to drown herself. The next day they stopped at the home of a peasant named Coudroyer. Josephine bewailed her lot unceasingly and complained she could not withstand the irresistible power of the wretched beggar. She begged to be allowed to sleep in a near-by room for she feared the cruel embraces of Castellan. But just as she tried to leave the room he approached her, seized her by her shoulders and she sank lifeless to the floor. Soon, at the command of the man, she arose, began counting the number of stairs and broke out into hysteric laughter. It was also noted by the spectators that she was incapable of feeling in all parts of her body.

The next morning she refused nourishment and continually called on the Virgin Mary for help. Castellan wanted to try out a new test of his powers over her and commanded her to roll around the floor on her knees; she obeyed. Tortured by the miseries of the maiden and embittered at the boldness with which the seducer displayed his power over the poor wretch, the people forcibly threw the beggar out of the house. Scarcely had the door closed behind him when Josephine fell like a corpse to the floor. Castellan was called back, made various signs over her and she recovered consciousness. They spent that night together.

The next day they continued their way. The inhabitants had not dared to restrain him from taking Josephine. Suddenly she came running back. Castellan had stopped to talk to a hunter and she had utilized the moment to flee from him. She begged to be hidden and to be freed from his power. She was returned to her father and from that time on did not appear to be completely sane.

Castellan was seized. They found out that he had been previously imprisoned for a similar crime. He would select subjects who were sympathetic to his hypnotic "passes" and then work his will on them. Twice he had had sexual intercourse with her when she was neither sleeping nor unconscious, but in a lethargic state; once when she was awake but had no conscious-

Mme. Chambige's Tragic Enchantment

ness of what was going on; and twice when she was completely unconscious. Castellan was condemned to twelve years of forced labor.

The case of Chambige was a very recent one and caused a great uproar in society.

Mme. Chambige was a very popular figure in society. She was well known for her good work as well as for her good heart. Happily married and the mother of three children, she should have been very contented. But one day she was found dead, a suicide. This inexplainable act caused great wonder among her friends until the contents of a letter she had left behind were made known to the public: "It is four years now that I have been under the influence of Monsieur X, and have committed acts with him for which I had the greatest disgust. When he is away I am in full possession of my normal senses, but as soon as he approaches I feel my will weaken and must do whatever he says. I can no longer face my children. I am taking the only way out."

As a last case we have a very curious one that occurred in England in the nineteenth century. A passionate lover, named Henry Prince, infatuated his feminine contingent into believing that it was possible for him to devirginize a beautiful maiden, Miss Paterson, in a public assembly of his adherents in the "Sanctuary of Love" which he had founded. He indeed announced that he would in the power of God take a virgin to wife, not with fear and shame in a secret place, but publicly in the light of day and in the presence of both sexes. It was God's will for him to take her, and he would ask permission of no one, not even the chosen girl herself. Which one he would take, he said not. The virgins should thus hold themselves in readiness for his favors.

This unique ceremony was actually performed in public! What a revolution in the thoughts and feelings of the mixed audience was necessary for him to accomplish such an outrageous spectacle. Such a daring scheme can be understood only by the powerful hypnotic personality of Prince who worked on the receptive minds of his carefully chosen adherents to such an extent that nothing he did was considered wrong or evil. Indeed the saint drew his company even closer to himself by means of this public copulation! We leave it to the imagination of the reader to draw the inference of his physical powers and ability to enamour the virgins into permitting such gross liberties with them.

CHAPTER NINE

MAGIC DRINKS—MAGIC INVOCATIONS—MAGIC APHRODISIACS

§ 1

Love-Charms of the Egyptians

In his analysis of the papyri in the British Museum, Berthelot notes that magic charms and formulas of invocations form a significant part of these manuscripts. He cites numerous formulas in which the names of Isis, Osiris, Hermes, Horus, Serapis, Mithras, Iao, Adonai, etc., are blended with one another. "These definite formulas," he says, "are for the invocation of a spirit who appears in the form of a child or an old woman, the servant of Apollonius of Tyana, and gives in the dream supernatural information, talismans against demons, ghosts, diseases and pains, magic drinks to acquire love or friendship." Berthelot further proves that the papyri contain a wealth of details that bears close resemblance to the symbolic customs of magicians and alchemists.

Actually almost all the papyri found today in the museums and libraries of Europe are derived from the temple at Memphis and correspond to those in the Louvre which came from the same source. This is explained by the fact that the magic books in Egypt belonged to the kings. They were consulted only in cases of the most urgent necessity and then were used only by the actual advisers of the Pharaoh, the priests and savants. Thus the papyrus W at the Leyden Museum contains a formula for mystic ink for writing magic formulas, which is compounded by mixing seven perfumes and seven flowers.

The following formulas are also to be found in this important papyrus: Magic ceremonies aided by love considered of great thaumaturgical power. Applications of Agathocles for creating love-dreams. Formula for separating a man from his wife. Charms that will cause glowing love.

Such instances prove that the art of magic drinks and invocations was known to the Egyptians reaching back to the oldest of times. We shall find such formulas in Greece and Italy.

§ 2

INVOCATIONS AMONG THE ARABIANS AND GREEKS

Plotinus explains in his *Enneads* the power of magic "by the sympathy which things have for one another." The artificial magic of the magician consists in uniting those natures which have mutual inherent attractions.

Ibn Khaldun explains magic in almost the same

fashion. "In magic," he says, "one spirit is joined to another; in the talismanic art it is a spirit that is joined to a body." This should be compared with the definition of Plotinus: "True magic is the friendship which, with its opposite, hatred, rules the world. The first magician whom man asks for advice and for aid with love-drinks is love!"

Concerning the objection made by Porphyrius and many others after him, that the magicians merely mouth words at their labors that signify naught, Jamblichus answers that men are certainly unable to understand the significance of many words but that they are known to the gods, the originators of the formulas and hence are necessary to the mystic practices of magicians. It should not be thought that these words, no matter how barbaric they may appear, are the inventions of evil spirits. If this were so, it would be a mere matter of using any words from a foreign language whereas it is a fact that only when the true magic words are used can there be any possibility of divine intervention.

§ 3

INSEPARABILITY OF MAGIC AND LOVE

HOW TO WIN BACK LOST LOVE

The echoes of this belief resounded through the centuries of the love-poets. We hear the voice of "The Enchantress" in the second idyll of Theocritus:

> "Where are those laurels? Bring them, Thestylis — and
>   the love charms too.
> Wreath the cauldron with a crimson fillet of fine wool;
> That I may cast a fire-spell on the man I love,
> Who now for twelve whole days, the wretch, has
>   never come this way,
> Nor even knows whether I be alive or dead, nor once
> Has he knocked at my doors, ah cruel! Can it be that
>   Love
> And Aphrodite have borne off his roving heart else-
>   whither?
> To Timagetos' wrestling school tomorrow I will go,
> And find him and reproach him with the wrong he
>   is doing me.
> But now by fire-magic will I bind him. Thou, O Moon,
> Shine fair; for to thee softly, dread Goddess, will
>   I chant,
> And to infernal Hekate, at whom the very whelp

Shudder, as she goes between the dead men's tombs
   and the dark blood.
Hail, awful Hekate! and be thou my helper to the
   end,
Making these charms prove no less potent than the
   spells of Circe
Or of Medea, or the gold-haired sorceress Perimede.
My magic wheel, draw home to me the man I love!"

Melissa has been jilted by her lover Charinus who now spends all his time in the arms of her rival, Simike. She confides her sorrow to her dear friend, Bacchis. "If perchance you are acquainted with an old woman who is expert in the mysteries of the Thessalian art of making men passionate and of desiring those whom they may even hate, then you will confer on me a great favor if you will bring me to her. I will gladly give her my clothes and jewelry if she can by her art make Charinus fall back into my arms again and make in my place Simike hateful to him." And it chanced that Bacchis knew just the magician Melissa needed. "We have here, my dear, an expert and talented enchantress. She reconciled Phanias to me when he had gotten into the habit of avoiding me at night. After he had avoided me for four months and I had despaired forever of his lost embraces she caused him by an enchantment to come back to me as enamoured as ever."

The witches of Thessaly, as we note here, were held in great regard; nothing, according to Lucian, could withstand the power of their magic drinks. They were fully able to transform a Cato into an Adonis and a Lucrecia into an Aspasia and of making the aged hot and fiery for love and perfectly capable of satisfying their lust.

Tibullus writes to Delia: "Three times must you repeat the song and then three times must you spit on the threshold of your bedchamber: this charm will render your husband scornful of the reports of his spies; even if he saw me with his own eyes lying in bed with you, he would still not believe it possible." The sly poet added: "But heed well, Delia, for the magic works only for my own person: if you grant your charming favors to another man your husband will see all; the enchantress has made this magic potent for myself alone."

In spite of his idiocies with Corinna and Neera, Ovid placed no trust in the power of the love-charms. "In vain," he says, "are the hippomanes torn from a young mare applied; in vain the herbs of Medea; in vain the magic charms of the Marsians; nothing can produce or retain love but love itself." But, alas! this was only a mood!

In the midst of all the superstitious beliefs of the middle ages and even in the sixteenth and seventeenth centuries we encounter time and time again this belief in the power of magic charms. Lovers have called and always will call on the supernatural powers, consult the witches or the modern equivalents, gypsy fortune tellers

Aphrodisiac Magic Drinks

and the like, by magic drinks, wear star-encrusted rings, and similar good-luck talismans: for magic and love are inseparable.

§ 4

Compounding of Aphrodisiac Magic Drinks
Modern Optherapy
Old Man Young Again   Old Woman Young Again

Magic drinks usually consisted of liquids, powders and salves, for the purpose of increasing the supernatural power of the magician. "There were usually to be found in these compounds," says Plytoff, "valerian, ivy, mallow, cypress, as well as snakes, owls and toads. The aphrodisiac love-philtres were usually compounded of vultures' heads, wolves' brushes, ashes of pictures of canonized saints, hair, and so forth. All of these varied components had to be thoroughly mixed in a special fashion after they had undergone the usual ceremonial rites."

Besides these bizarre ingredients, two substances took a decisive place in the fabrication of the love-philtres: sperm and menstrual blood.

The quite peculiar logic of their procedures naturally led the sorcerers to especially strange conclusions. In their studies in the field of love-drinks and talismans, they imparted an exceedingly important rôle to animals according to their temperament as observed in sexual directions.

In the formulas which they considered irresistible the main place was taken by such substances as the heart of a dove, the testicles of a cony (rabbit) and of a cock, the liver of a hyena, the eyes of cats in heat and similar phantasmagoric ingredients.

Real hecatombs of animals were found in the recesses of magicians when the animals were in rut. These creatures would meet in the starry nights, the domesticated pets on streets and roofs, and the wild animals under the shadowy branches of the great forests. Mad in the embrace of sexual frenzy, they easily fell into the rapacious hands of the greedy magicians.

Alas! thrice alas! for all-too-imprudent katzenjammer unable to hide the heat of their passion, the enamoured turtle-doves, the hyena boasting of his victory over his love-rival. Their skins, entrails and genitals must form the infernal pharmacopœia of the alchemistic laboratories. From their entrails are manufactured salves, powders, and pills. From their skins are prepared mystic writings, secret words, cabalistic figures and the like; such amulets are to be sold at unbelievably high prices to the gullible victims.

But it should not be imagined that such practices have disappeared in this modern and enlightened age! We ourselves have very often seen in the *corridas* of the arena of Madrid, Seville, Granada and Cordova how the virilities of the bulls are worshipfully adored by passionate Spanish gamins, old gentlemen, and even by beautiful young women, and how they very cynically speak

Modern Opotherapy

of the aphrodisiac effect it will have on those who are fortunate enough to enjoy them.

Since the days that Brown-Séquard, the famous English physician, turned his attention in his old age to his impotent bladder and cured the weakness of his urinations by his well-known method, the science of opotherapy (opos-juice) was discovered: testicle-juice for the old who would be young again, juice of the gray nerve-substances for simpletons, juice for the weak and ailing bones.

But it did not stop with that! It is well known how women mentally as well as physically suffer at the dread approach of the menopause when they must say farewell to their sexual life. There are prepared for their especial delectation costly brews of the ovaries of rabbits and thus young maidens are made of old matrons. We have heard this precious euphemism sung aloud on the streets of Damascus by a flower-seller: "Salih hamatak" (Satisfy your mother-in-law)!

We will now give some special cases of the formulas to show how little the opotherapeutic pharmacopœia differs from the magical pharmacopœia.

§ 5

Hindu Love-Charms — Magical Pharmacopoeia
Magic Drinks for Increasing Sexual Vigor
Miraculous Aphrodisiacs

Just as with talismans and amulets, the magic drugs have a history reaching far back to the most ancient of times. Vatsya Yana, the famed author of *Kama Sutra*, recounts many means of attaining the most desirable qualities: good looks, excellencies, youths and liberality.

Love Charms: An ointment made of the tabernamontana coronaria, the costus speciosus or arabicus, and the flacourtia cataphracta has magical effects on other persons.

If a fine powder is made of the above plants and applied to the wick of a lamp which is made to burn with the oil of blue vitriol, the black pigment or lamp-black produced therefrom has the effect of making a person look lovely when applied to the eyelashes.

The oil of the hogweed, the echites putescens, the sarina plant, the yellow amaranth and the leaf of the nymphæ if applied to the body has the same effect.

A black pigment from the same plants produces a similar effect.

By eating the powder of the nelumbrium speciosum, the blue lotus, and the mesna roxburghii, with ghee and honey, a man becomes lovely in the eyes of others.

Magical Pharmacopœia

The above things together with the tabernamontana coronaria, and the xanthochymus pictorius, if used as an ointment, produce the same results.

If the bone of a peacock or of an hyena be covered with gold and tied on the right hand it makes a man lovely in the eyes of other people.

In the same way, if a bead made of the seed of the jujube or of the conch shell be enchanted by the incantations mentioned in the Arthavana Veda, or by the incantations of those well skilled in the science of magic, and tied on the hand, it produces the same results described above.

Subjecting women: If a man after anointing his lingam with a mixture of the powders of the white thorn apple, the long pepper and the black pepper and honey engages in sexual union with a woman he subjects her to his will.

The application of a mixture of the leaf of the plant vatodbhranta, of the flowers thrown on a human corpse when carried out to be burnt, and of the powders of the bones of the peacock and of the jiwanjiva bird produces the same effect.

The remains of a kite which has died a natural death, ground into powder, and mixed with cowach and honey has also the same effect.

Anointing oneself with an ointment made of the plant embilica myrabolans has the power of subjecting women to one's will.

If a man cuts into small pieces the sprouts of the vajnasunhi plant, and dips them into a mixture of red arsenic and sulphur, and then dries them seven times, and applies this powder mixed with honey to his penis, he can subjugate a woman to his will directly that he has had sexual union with her, or, if by burning the sprouts at night and looking at the smoke, he sees a golden moon behind, he will then be successful with any woman; or if he throws some of the powder of these same sprouts mixed with the excrements of a monkey upon a maiden, she will not be given in marriage to anyone else

If the pieces of the arris root are dressed with the oil of the mango, and placed for six months in a hole made in the trunk of a sisu tree, and are then taken out and made up into an ointment, and applied to the penis, this serves as the means of subjecting women.

Increased Sexual Vigor: A man obtains sexual vigor by drinking milk mixed with sugar, the root of the uchchata plant, the piper chaba, and licorice.

Drinking milk mixed with sugar and having the testicle of a ram or goat boiled in it, is also productive of sexual vigor.

The drinking of the juice of the hedysarum gangeticum, the kuili, and the kshirika plant mixed with milk, produces the same effect.

The seed of the long pepper along with the seeds of the sanseviera roxburghiana and the hedysarum gangeticum plant, all pounded together, and mixed with milk, is productive of a similar effect.

According to ancient authors, if a man pounds the

Magic Drinks for Increasing Sexual Vigor

seeds or roots of the trapa bispinosa, the kasurika, the tuscan jasmine, and licorice, together with the kshirakapoli (a kind of onion) and puts powder into milk mixed with sugar and ghee, and having boiled the whole mixture on a moderate fire, drinks the paste so formed, he will be able to enjoy innumerable women.

In the same way if a man mixes rice with the eggs of the sparrow and having boiled this in milk, adds to it ghee and honey and drinks as much of this as is necessary it will produce the same effect.

If a man takes the outer covering of sesamum seeds and soaks them with the eggs of sparrows and then having boiled them in milk, mixed with sugar and ghee, along with the fruits of the trapa bispinosa and the kasurika plant, and adding to it the flour of wheat and beans, and then drinks this composition, he can enjoy many women.

If ghee, honey, sugar and licorice in equal quantities, the juice of the fennel plant, and milk are mixed together, this nectar-like composition is said to be holy, provocative of sexual vigor, a preservative of life, and sweet to the taste.

Pierre Mora gives the following formula: "Pulversize the heart of a dove, the liver of a sparrow, the womb of a swallow, the kidney of a hare, mix them in equal parts with their dried blood and eat a drachma two or three times."

The following formula is taken from the *Livre des secrets de magie*: "Capture a living toad. On a Friday before the rising of the sun, at the hour of Venus, hang it by its hind legs in a flue. Pulverize it dry, wrap it in paper, place it for three days under an altar and fetch it on the third. If a mass is read on this altar then it will make all the women run after you."

The following is very highly recommended: "Burn three hairs plucked from the sexual parts and three more from under the left armpit. Place the resulting powder in a food to be eaten by the person whom you are desirous of falling in love with you and that person will never leave you."

This philtre is also praised by many magicians as being unsurpassable for the above purpose: "The brain of a cat and of a lizard; the menstrual blood of a whore; human semen; the womb of a bitch in heat which has been denied the companionship of dogs; the entrails of a hyena and the left skull-bone of a toad."

According to Cornelius Agrippa if a person wishes to prepare love-philtres he must take those members, in part or in whole, in which the sexual desires are present, and from those animals which indulge most in coition and at those periods of the year in which they are in heat: the dove, the turtle-dove, the sparrow, the swallow.

Albertus Magnus assures us that evergreen pulverized together with earthworm will excite love in men and women if mixed with meat in their foods.

He similarly describes the high properties of polygonum which are strongly excitant and lend great strength

Miraculous Magic Aphrodisiacs

in coition. Verbena will also do the same and its juice "faire beaucoup de sperme."

Magnus's magic book mentions drugs which can serve with success but only when Mercury is in ascendancy: from the 23rd to the 30th Mondays. Complicated rules and formulas are also necessary for complete success.

We give a few of the formulas which Albert praises as infallible and as potent to the nth degree.

The first refers to hippomanes. It apparently suffices for just a bit of this substance to be swallowed in a liquid or food. If it takes place on a Friday and in an hour favorable to Venus then the effect is infallible.

Second formula: On Friday in Spring let some of your blood dry in a little basin together with the two testes of a hare and the liver of a dove. Pulverize thoroughly. Give three times one-half drachma to the person in whom you are interested and the latter will never cease loving you.

Third formula: Pluck on the evening before Midsummer's Day, the plant enula campana, dry and pulverize it with gray ambra and carry it for nine days next to the genital region. Then give some of it to the person by whom you want to be loved. The effect is miraculous.

In the second act of *Tristan and Isolde,* Wagner has the heroine describe the tempests which the love-philtre has aroused in her, in the following words:

> *"Of Frau Minne knowest full naught—*
> *Nor aught of her marvellous might—*

> Of courage's dauntless
> Mood the queen;
> O'er the world created
> Reigning supreme:
> Life and Death
> Subdued she hath,
> That from joys and sorrows she wove
> Changing all hatred to Love!
> The work of death
> Rashly and lightly I planned;
> Frau Minne took
> All the strength from my hand.
> The rescued one
> She held as pledge,
> Took o'er the work
> My heritage.
> Whatever she change,
> What she arrange,
> What she decide
> Where she may guide,
> Hers I am henceforth surely,
> Obeying her wants demurely!"

And Tristan, at the beginning of the third act, wounded to death, still under the mastery of the all-consuming drink, hurls his immortal "love-curse":

> "The maddening drink
> That my woes unbared,

> *Have I, myself,*
> *For my life prepared,*
> *From father's need,*
> *From mother's woe,*
> *From true love's fears*
> *That for ever flow,*
> *From laughter and weeping,*
> *Rapture and wound,*
> *I the elixir's*
> *Poison found!*
> *The drink I brew'd*
> *That woes contained,*
> *That rapture-quaffing*
> *To the dregs I drained—*
> Accurs'd the brew that I quaffed!"
> Accurs'd be the terrible draught—

§ 6

HUMAN BLOOD AND THE WITCHCRAFT OF LOVE

Berthelot recalls that according to Avicenna and other old alchemists human blood was actually used for the alchemistic and magic transformations and manifestations. In order to be convinced of the influence that human blood had in magic, and escpecially in the witchcraft of love, it is necessary to become acquainted with some of the alchemistic theories.

We are in possession of a fragment of instructions

given by Zosimus, an ancient arabic alchemist, to his feminine novice, Marie: "Know then that the menstrual blood can only be pure when it has been washed by the sperm of man. The uterus of the woman seeks the sperm of man, for the sperm which falls into the uterus modifies the blood and transforms it into a white scum. From this scum is formed the body of the issuing child. The menstrual blood is fortunate in encountering the sperm, since this has also been blood. When blood meets blood, they strive to join one another and thus both commingle."

The rôle of blood, and especially of menstrual blood, reaches amazing heights in the field of Sexual Magic. Magicians dried upon the loins of women cookies made of flour and their menstrual blood. This love-host, rooted and warmed in the passionate spirit of Satan, was sent to the male who had proven to be a recalcitrant lover. As soon as he had tasted of it he was seized by the strangest of lusts and desires. That was the return of love.

The *Breviary of Lovers* also imparts prime importance to blood in the field of love-philtres. Its use is given to many different forms: as sympathetic inks, drinks, etc. But it predicates the efficacy of the magic to a glowing belief, a pure desire, that must accompany all these magical operations.

And how many cases do our law-courts report of women who tried to force the issue with their lovers by secretly dropping some of their menstrual blood in the food and drink the quicker to prompt a proposal of marriage!

The case of Mlle. Jeanne who mixed half a cup of coffee with her stale menstrual blood is too nauseating a story to repeat here, if indeed it is not still warm in the reader's mind.

§ 7

Magical Love-Philtres

and

Talismans against Impotency

The number of magical love-philtres and talismans against impotency are myriad. Since impotency was very often considered the work of demons, recourse was usually taken to invocations.

We here give the almost complete text of an exorcism of devils from a man who had been made impotent by magic means: "May all the infernal power be extinguished within thee. Be thou free of all entanglements, bewitchments, and enchantments of Satan and his servants. May procreativity and favor be given thee so that thou canst honorably complete the sacred rites of marriage. The demons who have prepared and wrought this magic on thee must be gone from they person and they themselves become impotent, no matter where they be nor the pacts they may have concluded with magicians and witches against thee."

There formerly existed numerous rituals each having various versions. Thiers gives an enormous collection of them in his *Superstitions* and cites as particularly curious the ritual of Chartres dating about 1640.

The pious Khodja Omer Haleby Abu recommends the following treatment against impotency: "If you must conquer the impotency of another, bid him to prepare his pollutions and prayers. Then place the index finger of the right hand on the end of his Dkeur member, the left hand flat against his stomach and command him to gaze fixedly at you. Then lower your glance to that of the victim and speak to him in the spirit of the last two chapters of the Koran wherein you must say with a loud and commanding voice: "Go! from this moment on the magic spell is broken and you are no longer impotent."

In case of failure this operation is repeated three times in a period of three weeks.

In order to procure such cures one need not necessarily be a magician. A proof of this may be here pertinent. Many years ago we were in Biskra. The Arabian who served us as a guide told us that a Jewish magician with whom he had quarrelled had enchanted him in revenge and that since that time he was impotent. The following advice was given him:

"It is Eblis himself (the destroying angel of the Koran) who has bound you; Allah alone can release you. For seven days must you twice daily visit the mosques, genuflecting with your face towards the east

Talismans Against Impotency

and pronounce the holy formula, the incomparable prayer: *La ilaha illa allaha, Mohammed rasul allachi.* During this period you must not approach your women, but must leave them in the greatest of freedom possible. On the evening of the seventh day select the one whom you most favor and pray once more before you approach her, for the prayer renews the physical powers and the moral state. If you follow these precepts to the letter the spell that the Jew has thrown over you will be broken and you will be a man again."

All these rules were carefully followed by the Arabian and on the evening of the seventh day he again found delight in the embrace of his favorite: the spell was broken; he was cured.

That suggestion plays the largest possible part in the cure of the most frequent kind of impotency, psychic impotency, is very well known. It is this fact that explains many of the tales of cures of impotency by magic means.

For the man, unconditioned trust and a certain naïve devotion to his task are indeed necessary for the practice and completion of sexual intercourse. Preoccupation, lack of confidence, or embarrassment may lame the loins of the man. It is well known that in men who are busily occupied in spiritual and mental tasks a certain sexual incapacity appears, because throughout their marital labors scientific ideas are always flying through their heads. Thus Grimaux de Ceaux and Saint-Ange describe a case of a very famous mathematician who was always kept from completing the embrace because at that very moment problems of geometry and calculus would come into his mind, his entire body would be automatically shunted from the labor of Venus to the solution of $\iiint_R^\infty \rho\, d\rho\, d\theta\, dz$

Another interesting case is told by Hammond. A young prestidigitator whose thoughts were greatly engrossed by his work was suddenly taken with a deep sexual longing, after the end of his performance at a theatre. But he was never able to satisfy his desires for just as he would engage in intercourse a technical trick of cards would come to his mind and destroy not only his desire but his ability to complete the coition. This failure of discharge had as a result the awakening of fear in him that he would be unable to attain the sexual goal in future coitions, and this fear became the reality, no matter how often he tried to conquer it.

CHAPTER TEN
SEX TALISMANS AND AMULETS

§ 1

Phallic Talismans
of
Classical and Medieval Times

IN ALL ages have there been amulets and talismans. The Temples and palaces of ancient Assyria were decorated with colossal images of animals which served as talismanic forms. Lenormant in his epic-making work *Magic, Prophecy, and the Secret of Sciences of Ancient Chaldea* cites innumerable instances of talismanic luck-charms either found in the ruins of their temples or mentioned in their literature.

From the most ancient times, indeed from the very moment that the graphic arts attempted to imitate the works of nature, the coarse and awkward imitation of the clumsily modelled or carved phallus has been a favorite talisman of good-luck to mankind. With the refinements of Greek art the phallus became the fashion. The phalli were decorated with gaily colored ribbons, had a pair of wings, and were used as a leading motif in all the familiar objects of the household. The beautiful hetæræ of Athens and Corinth wore them about their necks and were soon followed by the haughty patricians of Rome.

For untold centuries the lingam filled this rôle in India. Indeed the custom was so strong that the missionaries found they could make no headway at all if they insisted on the people giving up their charms. The Jesuits solved the problem by having them wear a cross upon each of their penis-amulets.

During the Middle Ages the erotic art of the talisman became exceedingly complicated. The Latin traditions, the oriental romanticism, the Olympic heights, all became mixed with a cloak of Christian mysticism and Pagan mythology. Olympic gods, archangels, demons, phalli, and cunni, sported themselves on the necks and garments of men and women.

§ 2

Modern Erotic Talismans
Astrology and Secret Properties of Jewels

Today the talisman enjoys as much power and pomp as it ever did. True it does not take the form of wearing an image of a penis about the neck but there are other and less obvious symbolisms sported by innocent men and women. One need but read the advertisements of certain newspapers and magazines to convince oneself of the truth of the above statement.

Pass by the window of any window-displayed jewelry establishment and the reader will be amazed to find

Modern Erotic Talismans

what a large proportion of the stock consists of talismans and amulets. There among all the rings, armbands, brooches, tiepins, etc., appear certain bits of jewelry of strange form and baroque composition which appear to be of little value to the eyes of the profane, but of momentous importance to the sympathetic gaze of the initiate. There are the four-leaf clovers which will bring success in all undertakings; the sapphire on which are engraved secret and powerful arabesque formulas; the irresistible rings which make even the coldest of beauties humble and submissive; the abraxas, the conqueror of fate; the armbands which retain life; the esoteric brooches with cabalistic signs and images; the seal with its poor imitation of the seal of Solomon; and a thousand and one objects of a similar genre, not forgetting the tiny coral-hand that protects a person from bewitchments.

Let us also not forget the secret stock of the jeweler, his erotic and sometimes openly obscene talismans. Especially popular with the men is the ring with the two lovers embracing in the notorious posture of "69": this will make a Casanova of any man. The women, especially the passionate and lewd ones, are entranced with a large assortment of godemichés, bejewelled and carved in many fashions.

It should not be imagined that this medieval armor is bought by lovers only as curios and strange trash. An unimaginably great number of believers are to be found who place faithful trust in the talismans and amulets for the attainments of their dreams and desires. In no other way can the immense number of such objects sold yearly be satisfactorily explained.

In cases where the believer is unable to find the particular object he desires among the wide stock, there are jewelers who will prepare the talismans for him according to the rigid laws of the art. Stones or seals will be made according to the hour, day, month and year of birth of the purchaser; according to his type, color, temperament, position; according to his need for luck, power, fame, fortune, love, and the like.

The astrologist Gévingey was such a jeweler and carried his show-window on his fingers; they were covered with rich and strange rings and he would say to the ubiquitous curious spectator: "You examine my valuables, monsieur. They are of three metals, gold, platinum and silver. This ring bears a scorpion, the sign under which I was born. That with its two accoupled triangles, one pointing downward and the other upward, reproduces the image of the macrocosm, the seal of Solomon, the grand pentacle. As for the little one you see here," he would go on, showing a lady's ring set with a tiny sapphire between two roses, "that is a present from a person whose horoscope I was good enough to cast."

These lines are sufficient to prove that the preparation of these special objects is a task demanding the combination of excellent workmanship and a thorough knowledge of theoretical astrology. Thus it is not surprising to find that these workers in jewels are thorough savants in the hidden properties of metals, the secret formulas of the magic books, the mysteries of the cabala, a knowledge of comparative religions and a thorough acquaintance with the esoteric myths of ancient times. Nor will it prove so surprising to the reader to find that the art of the talisman, indeed all white magic, is an exact science to its initiates.

§ 3

CLASSIFICATIONS OF TALISMANS

Talismans are of two kinds: simple and compound.

The simple talismans, as is suggested by their name, consist of only one substance, that is, of one metal. A ring of silver, an agate, a pearl necklace, a diamond,— these are simple talismans.

The compound talismans are quite differently developed. Their name shows that they are the result of thousands of combinations of which we have spoken before.

The talismans may be either metallic, mineral, vegetable or animal, according to the applied substances or objects.

They may be cabalistic; that is, formed of characters

whose combination possesses magic power. Thus the well-known abracadabra triangle

```
A B R A C A D A B R A
 A B R A C A D A B R
  A B R A C A D A B
   A B R A C A D A
    A B R A C A D
     A B R A C A
      A B R A C
       A B R A
        A B R
         A B
          A
```

has degenerated in our time into a mere exclamation of nonsense or surprise, and the very people who use the expression would be most greatly astonished if they discovered that it was inescapably connected with witchcraft and other occult powers!

Written in this fashion on parchment and placed next to the heart, it was considered a sure protection against the spells and enchantments of witches. It was the astrologic talisman of Catherine de Medici, upon which is depicted the nude princess between the symbols of the bull and the ram, carrying in one hand an arrow and in the other a pierced flaming heart inscribed with secret symbols. Thus, mathematical talismans possess power which rests in geometrical figures or numbers. Thus, blasphemous talismans are so called if divers profanations are neccesary to consecrate them, as in the case of an alraune, that demonic invention of an unknown uncanny lunatic.

The talismans are also divided into active and passive. In love the active talismans influence the spirit or mind of the desired person. The passive talismans are those whose activity is limited to the effect of the invocations, such as magic philtres or cryptic pronouncements which guard against all kinds of enchantments.

§ 4

Talismanic Formulas of the Magic Books

Their Wondrous Rôle in Love and Sex

To appease the curiosity of the reader we will first of all cite some of the formulas and magic secrets which concern love talismans and which are based mostly on the extraordinary magic-books of Albertus Magnus.

Nichomar is superb for conquering enemies and for making oneself beloved by others. It is almost identical with alabaster. It is white and gleaming; salves are made of it to perfume the biers of the dead.

In order to discover whether a wife is untrue to her husband or whether she loves another there must be used the galeriate gem which is like the cinnabar; it is found in Libya and in Brittany. It comes in three colors: black, yellow, and green, which reflect white. It cures dropsy and stops diarrhœa. Avicenna declares that if this gem is pulverized and if a woman washes herself with it, she will have to urinate immediately if she is unchaste; but if she is pure in heart as well as body she will not have to urinate.

If one wishes to force love and make two persons enamoured of each other the echite gem, also called eagle-stone, because it is usually found in eyries, is used. It has a pronounced purple color; it hides in another stone which echoes when it is tapped. The ancients believed that when worn on the left arm it would awaken love in man or woman.

Those who wish to guard their virginity must employ the aid of the saune gem which is found on the island of the same name.

The following animal-talismans have had an invincible belief for ages. There is often found on the heads of studs and breeding-mares tufts of skins, of which a curious use is made for purposes of love. When these tufts of skin, called hippomanes by the ancients, are obtained, they must be dried in a new earthen pot in a stove, from which bread has just been baked. If it is then worn on the person and is touched by the desired lover, success will surely result.

The marrow of beef also possesses wondrous powers. "Take the marrow found in the left foot of an ox," says Albertus Magnus, "make a pomade of it, mix it with common gray ambergris and powdered cyprus. Wear this pomade, and from time to time let the woman, whom you are desirous of making enamoured of you,

Substances Used in Elixir

smell it and she will infallibly learn to adore you."

Animals play a large rôle in the compounding of talismans, love-philtres and erotic drugs, not only in the magic books of the occultists of the middle ages but also in the recipes of country-magicians. We find definite traces of this superstition in India, ancient and modern.

An engoldened bone of a peacock or hyena made fast to the hand makes the wearer desirous in the eyes of all spectators. The same success is achieved by fastening a wreath of zyziphus vulgaris to the wrist, accompanied by the charms given in the *Atharva Veda* (Book of Magic Invocations) or by a clever magician.

The ten animal substances used by the hermetic philosophers for the preparation of the elixir were: hair, skull, brain, gall, blood, milk, egg, urine, horns and mother-of-pearl.

Hair was the most important of these substances. It has always played, as it still does today, a significant rôle in love and sex. Beliefs in the virtue of hair are so widespread that it is impossible to give even a short account of all the superstitions that are bound up in it. However, they are all derived from the fact that hair is a part of the person and is as influential a substitute as the whole being.

In this connection we are reminded of an incident concerning a newly-married young woman acquaintance of ours. Upon accidently ripping her marriage robe she was astounded in finding out that the seams contained a real collection of hair. She found there all possible shades of color: blond, brown, black, red, in all sorts of nuances. She sought for the key to the puzzle high and low and finally discovered that it was the dressmaker's fault. When a marriage robe is prepared in a dressmaking establishment, girls who are acquainted with the dressmaker beg her to place a lock of their hair in the seam of the marriage garment. This hiding place has the infallible property of procuring each of the fortunate girls a Prince Charming within the course of one year.

§ 5

Symbolic Jewelry

Those confusing aids of feminine beauty — jewelry — have a symbolic significance and a language all their own.

Let us first examine rings:

> Worn on index finger = I would like to get married.
> Worn on middle finger = I am already in love.
> Worn on ring finger = Useless; married or engaged.
> Worn on little finger = I want to remain single.

Somewhat similar is the case with armbands, slave-bracelets and the like:

> On right arm = Free of all and every entanglement.
> On both or on left wrist = Married.
> On the left only = Engaged.

Is not the marriage ring a talisman? Indeed, if the expression is allowable, is it not the typical talisman? It should consist of unmixed metal: "May your love be as pure as this gold!" Hence it was formerly preferred to make the rings of fine gold. The names of the married couple, or at least their initials, are to be engraved in the inner part of the ring. In order to definitely consecrate its power and to place it under the ægis of God, the Catholic Church has promulgated a solemn formula which is pronounced by the priest and by which he prays that God "send his spirit on the ring so that the one who wears it will be inspired by the spirit of divine protection."

In some countries such occult influence is placed on the marriage ring that the moment in which it is changed and the manner in which it is placed on the finger becomes an object of the greatest attention. "That very minute in which the groom gives the ring to his young bride before the priest," says the *Dictionnaire infernal*, according to an old magic book, "is of supreme importance. If the man halts when the ring is only at the tip of the finger without its going over the second joint, then the wife will be the mistress of the house, but if it goes over the finger at one onslaught, then the man will be the lord and master of the household."

It is curious to note that in many superstitious countries the brides will employ various deceits to prevent the marriage ring from passing the second joint. Crooking the finger is the most common method.

§ 6

Phallic Monuments
in
Ireland United States India
Amatory Pilgrimages

There is one class of talismans which is altogether unique because its objects are immovable and usually found in inaccessible places. Accordingly, it is necessary to make a special pilgrimage to them if one desires a small part of their power by touching or embracing them. Such talismans were formerly certain statues, monoliths, gigantic granite lingams in India and the phalli of the Greek and Roman temples.

Such a talisman is to be found in the castle Blarney in Ireland. In a corner of this historic castle there is a stone bearing the date of 1703 which attracts thousands of pilgrims every year who kiss it in order to be granted its two qualities: the gift of eloquence and the power of winning the heart of the beloved.

It would require a volume in itself to classify and describe all such monuments, enchanted stones and mountains, fetish trees and woods, and similar places which abound in most countries. Indeed, we would be bold enough to say that there does not exist a locality which has not some talisman endowed by local or national tradition with mystic or magic power.

Indeed, in so unexpected a place as the campus of a

Amatory Pilgrimages 157

midwestern co-educational college in the United States of America, a perpendicular block of stone, with two smaller rocks acting as its base, is rooted in the ground. The campus tradition is that the co-ed who kisses the pinnacle of this stone, which resembles a phallus no less obvious than the lingam-blocks of the Hindus, will get married within a year and will have many children! Photographs of girls in their osculatory obeisance to this phallic symbol are relatively common.

§ 7

Metals Sacred to Venus
Arabian Love-Magnet

We shall now pass to the subject of metals. These have played a symbolic rôle in ancient times as we learn from the works of the hermetic philosophers. We shall treat only of those that are connected with sex.

According to Artefius, copper comes from Venus; its nature is like that of Venus. The Greek named it *aphrodite* and *aphrondon,* and the Chaldeans *bilati* after their Venus of that name.

The bluish gleam of Venus, the evening and the morning star, is reminiscent of the color of the cupric salts of the metal of that name coming from Cypris, the holy island of the goddess Cypris, from whose Greek name Venus is taken. A majority of writers connect Cypris with the Egyptian deity Hathor, whose polyformed colors recall the blue, green, yellow and red derivatives of copper.

Zosimus quotes an interesting legend about the myth of tin. "In the occident," says this savant, "there is a liquid source of tin. The people of the vicinity sacrifice a virgin to the god of this mine in order to entice him to come to the fount; he rushes forward to follow her, and the young people in ambuscade belabor him with axes so that they can cut him into bars."

The mysterious power of the magnet also fell to the attention of the Arabians. They believed that if they used it to darken their eyelids, they would infallibly draw the love of the person they adored.

In a certain sense brimstone also appears to be consecrated to Venus. In his treatise on brimstone Schuetzenberger declares: "The cult of Venus, the goddess of beauty, ruled in those places where sulphuric water was obtained. Even today in Italy next to almost every source of brimstone there is a chapel dedicated to a saint who bears the neme Venera, Venerea, Venerina, according to local usage. The etymology is clear: these chapels are ancient heathen temples which were changed into Christian monuments and the holy Venera is none other than the pagan Venus. Was it not at Milo that the beautiful statue of Venus, the masterpiece of ancient art, was found?"

§ 8

SECRET PROPERTIES OF GEMS

IN PROVINCE OF SEX

STONES AND SINS   NATURAL MAGIC

Gems have always played a significant rôle in love and still are an important element in almost every province of sex.

Among those who have occupied themselves with the secret properties of gems, the name of the famous Bishop Marbod stands foremost.

The language of gems, according to the opinions of occult savants, is as follows:

> White gems = purity, belief, truth.
> Red gems = power and fire.
> Blue gems = perseverance and happiness.
> Green gems = hope.
> Violet gems = love, passion.
> Orange gems = enthusiasm.
> Lilac gems = friendship.

Besides their symbolic language gems can become gracious interpreters of our sensations in the simplest manner. The alphabetic order completes the sensual gems. According to them, agate and carnelian stimu- and one may offer one's sweetheart a genuine acrostic made of gems:

$$\left.\begin{array}{l}\text{Ruby}\\\text{Opal}\\\text{Sapphire}\\\text{Emerald}\end{array}\right\} = \text{ROSE}$$

$$\left.\begin{array}{l}\text{Diamond}\\\text{Onyx}\\\text{Ruby}\\\text{Amethyst}\end{array}\right\} = \text{DORA}$$

Among other gems that form love emblems are counted:

the lapis lazuli = normal love
the carbuncle = burning love
the topaz = true and unselfish love
the pearl = permissible love
the smaragdine = first love
the turquoise = successful love

The cockstone, the eaglestone, and the amethyst, tell the initiate that the wearer is suffering the martyrdom of love.

Aristotle, Theophrastus, Pliny, all the sages of classical antiquity, attributed medical and magical power to

Stones and Sins 161

late, topaz consoles, jasper cures languor, hyacinth dispels insomnia, turquoise prevents falling, and amethyst combats drunkenness.

Catholic symbolism, in its turn, took over the idea behind precious stones and saw in them the emblems of Christian virtues. Thus sapphire represented the lofty aspirations of the soul, chalcedony charity, sard and onyx candor, beryl allegorized theological science, hyacinth humility, while the ruby appeased wrath and the emerald stood for incorruptible faith.

In medieval times, natural magic, which was merely the medicine of the time, ascribed a new meaning to gems. Porta celebrated an unknown stone, the alectorius, and declared its possessor invincible if it has been taken out of the stomach of a cock caponized four years before or if it has been ripped out of the ventricle of a hen. Porta further informs us that chalcedony wins law suits; that carnelian stops bloody flux and is "exceedingly useful to women who are sick of their flower;" that hyacinth protects against lightning and keeps away pestilence and poison; that topaz quells lunatic spells and passions; that turquoise suppresses melancholy, quartan fever and heart failure. He attests finally that sapphire preserves courage and keeps the members vigorous, while emerald, hung about one's neck, keeps away St. John's evil and breaks when the wearer is unchaste.

Antique philosophy, medieval Christianity, and sixteenth century magic thus did not agree on the specific virtues of every stone. Almost in every case the significations, more or less far-fetched, differ. The modern Dr. Johannès of Huysmans revised these beliefs, adopted and rejected great numbers of them and finally admitted new exceptions. According to him, amethyst does cure drunkenness, but it is moral drunkenness, pride; ruby relieves sex pressure; beryl fortifies the will; sapphire elevates the thoughts and turns them toward God.

In brief, he believes that every stone corresponds to a species of malady, and also to a class of sins; and he affirms that when we have chemically got possession of the active principle of gems we shall have not only antidotes but preventives. In the meantime he uses precious stones to formulate diagnoses of illness. He claims that when such or such a stone is placed in the hand or on the affected part of the victim a fluid escapes from the stone into his hands and that by examining this fluid he can tell what the ailment is. In this connection he declared that a woman whom he did not know came to him one day to consult him about a malady, pronounced incurable, from which she had suffered since childhood. He could not get any precise answers to his questions. He saw no signs of *venefice*. After trying out his whole array of stones he placed in her hand a lapis lazuli which according to him, corresponds to the sin of incest. He examined the stone.

"Your malady," he said, "is the consequence of an act of incest."

"Hm," she muttered. "I did not come here for confession." Nevertheless she finally admitted that her father had violated her before she attained the age of puberty!

§ 9

MANDRAKE OR MANDRAGORA
MORION OR DEATH-WINE
BABYLONIAN CHARM AGAINST STERILITY

We now come to the talismans belonging to the vegetable kingdom.

A crown of vervain is to all intent an excellent love charm. "The wearer," says Albertus Magnus, "will be very potent in coition, provided that he alone wears the crown."

But no matter how excellent vervain is, it cannot compare with the mandragora or mandrake. Mandragora is a solanine, a close relation to belladonna, whose roots assume the form of a human figure and whose upper part is entangled in a growth of baroque bones. Pythagoras gave it the name of "human-bodied." Bacon said of the mandrake that it was "a root whereof witches made an ugly image, giving it the form of a face on the top of the root." A wine made of the root had the effect of sending those that drank it into deep sleep, from which on awakening all manner of horrible things would be imagined. It has been called "the insane root which takes the reason prisoner."

Upon recovering from its effects a person would be wild and fearful, and often shrieking would accompany the awakening. Hence the saying, "shrieking like mandrakes."

> And shrieks like mandrakes torn out of the earth,
> That living mortals hearing them run mad.
> *Romeo and Juliet.*

In gathering or unearthing the root certain rites and ceremonies had to be performed, or it would not do its work well. An ancient writer, Josephus, says: "To gather ye mandragora, go forthe at dead of nyght and take a dogge or other animal and tye hym wyth a corde unto ye plante. Loose ye earth round about ye roote, then leave hym, for in his struggle to free hymself he will teare up ye roote whych by its dreadful cryes wyll kyll ye animal." Its "dreadfull crys" would be drowned by someone standing by, blowing a horn.

It was also used under the name of *morion* or "death wine" to render insensible those about to suffer torture. Hence under Roman rule, Jewish women would administer it to those who were being crucified. It would allay suffering and wrap the soul in night. It was on account of the occasional recovery of the crucified after they had been removed from the cross as dead that the Roman soldiers were ordered to mutilate the bodies before they were handed over to their friends for burial.

Its use for purposes of enchantment were also widely recognized. To the Babylonians and the Egyptians it was a charm against sterility, and was known to them as the "phallus of the field"; and to judge from the story connected with an episode in the life of Rachel (Genesis), the ancient Hebrews also believed it to possess a special virtue in this respect.

Even in modern times, the superstitious belief in the mandrake root has not been entirely obliterated. The gullible mujiks of pre-war Russia prize them as exceptional talismans that will bring them fame and fortune. They are given the name of *Adamova golova*, Adam heads. In China, mandragora is exceedingly expensive, the price varying with the plant's resemblance to the human form.

§ 10

Astrologic Talismans
The Planet of Love

The mystics and occultists place little significance on the more or less haphazard formulas of the magic books. They desire the genuine talismans to be constructed according to logical rules and that the effect wished for shall be suitable.

The most sensitive and undeniable influence in magic belong to the seven planets and hence man must have recourse to their power.

The talisman of each one of these planets must be

prepared on the hour and day that is favorable to it and must be made from the metal peculiar to it. It must also be compounded of the essences characteristic of the planet. In order for its good qualities to be retained, it must be guarded in a little sack of favorable colors. These favorable colors relate to the planet under whose auspices the magical work is completed.

The author of the *Cours d'Astrologie et des Clefs secrètes du Magnétisme* gives us a complete introduction into the origin and fabrication of a love-talisman.

"Let us assume," he says, "that I am enamoured of a woman and desire that my love be reciprocated, and turn to magic for aid. What will be my means?

"A talisman of love, which I will wear on my body so that it will make me master of the one I love. I want it to exert a powerful effect and hence I concentrate on those objects that will correspond to my desire: it must be formed of copper, since this is the metal of Venus, the mistress of love, and is favorable to the planet that rules the world of love. Thus my will is connected with the fundamental principal of my work.

"I will give it a circular form since the curves are dependent on the influence of Venus. I will complete the symbols peculiar to her, including all labor on the days and hours favorable to her and will consecrate it with proper customs. Then I shall place it in a little pouch of pure silk in the very colors of the planet and hang it about my neck. Each of these observances will impress my will, or better, my word, upon the talisman,

Astrologic Talismans

whose occult power assures me the desired success."

The main elements of this talisman consecrated to Venus are:

> Metal: copper
> Letter: H
> Note: D
> Day: Friday and the 23rd
> Numbers: 6 and 23
> Animal: the dove
> Flower: the rose
> Music: melody
> Jewel: green or reflecting green
> Color: green
> Odor: vivacious and alluring
> Tree: Olive tree

§ 11

Cryptic Letters and Numbers

The Seven Talismans of King Solomon

Magic Tables of Sex

Initial letters, and especial numbers, possess a hidden power, a magical ability, that has been known to man in all times. The first traces of a significance imparted to letters and numbers is to be found in Sepher Jezirah's *Book of Genesis*. From this can be understood how the practical Cabala arose which gave to these numbers and letters the power of changing the course of nature.

Certain words and names also possess magic force. A work of Zosimus speaks of the seven talismans which Solomon prepared from the seven planets. These talismans were nothing but flasks of amber in which he had imprisoned demons who were forced to serve him and who could not resist the nine magic letters which were written upon them.

According to Ibn Khaldun the word *simia* contains the most important hidden properties of the letters of the alphabet. "The word," he says, "just as the letters from which it is formed, grants to the spirit the ability to rule over nature and the world and as a result to determine the course of the created being." He adds:

"The practice of the talismanic art has helped us to learn the abilities of the friendly numbers. They are called friendly because the equal parts of a number, the half, the quarter, the fifth and the sixth, when added to one another, give equal sums. Those who occupy themselves with talismans assure us that these numbers possess the influence of forming a close connection and friendship between two individuals."

In relation to the properties of numbers and especially to that of the number 7, Aulus Gellius reports the following strange explanation of Varro regarding the influence of this number on the creation of man.

"When the male semen has been impelled into the

Cryptic Letters and Numbers 169

womb of the woman, their respective seeds unite and form themselves into a single organism. At the end of seven weeks, if the child is to be of the male sex, the head and spine are formed. In the seventh week, that is, on the forty-ninth day, the human fœtus is completed."

According to this curious theory man is but an arbitrary product of the mighty will of nature. Destiny depends on a combination of letters, words or numbers. From whose will, whose word, whose name? That is the cryptic problem. The universal secret consists in discovering of what syllables and letters the name of God is composed. Therein lies a tremendous power in which one can share from the very moment one is able to pronounce His name.

Such a mighty belief in the efficacy of numbers and names has naturally been felt in the field of sex. The numbers dedicated to Venus together with their mystic names are:

$$7 - \text{Ahea}$$
$$49 - \text{Haghiel}$$
$$157 - \text{Kedemel}$$
$$1252 - \text{Ben Seraphim}$$

The table of the numbers of Venus on the following page is one of the most effective talismans of love. Engraved on a silver plate, which represents the goddess as Venus Fortunata, it creates harmony, union, a great favorite with women, helps reception, prevents sterility, and renders one the equal of seven men during copulation. This is the magic table:

22	47	16	41	10	35	4
5	23	48	17	42	11	29
30	6	24	49	18	36	12
13	31	7	25	43	19	37
38	14	32	1	26	44	20
21	39	8	33	2	27	45
46	15	40	9	34	3	28

§ 12

Practical Power of Belief in Talismans

The transcendental value of talismans and amulets is equal to that of prayer. The sceptic can expect naught from it. Only the true believer will find the mystic meaning.

The savage, grasping his *gri-gri,* throwing himself upon the European bayonets in the firm belief that nothing can be greater than his charm, at least creates from this illusion an inscrutable power which has more than once repulsed the best-trained troops of the most civilized world.

It is less different with the meek and suppliant husband of a virago who suddenly finds in his hands the magic power of making himself master of the household. He rids himself of his inferiority complex by means of an amulet considered absurd by sceptics but held priceless by him. Or the shy and timid young men who become imitating Casanovas after kissing the blarney stone.

Whom does it harm? And what comfort and pleasure is to be derived from a belief in mystic talismans, none can say. Obviously, it should be no less than the comfort and pleasure that true believers receive in prayer to an invisible **God.**

CHAPTER ELEVEN

SEX LANGUAGES AND SYMBOLS

§ 1

THE LANGUAGE OF FLOWERS

CHARTS

FLOWERS have always been emblems and symbols to the eager eyes of lovers. Even today the hesitant maiden plucks the petals from the daisy to the tune of: "he loves me, he loves me not!" The answer of the flowers is awaited like that of some divine oracle.

But before all, the flowers spoke most gallantly in that chivalric period when "knighthood was in flower." If a lady placed a crown of white marguerites on the head of a proud knight who worshipped her, it meant: "I will take heed of your avowal..." And without any other encouragement it was a kind of delicate refusal, a simple assumption of veneration without further hopes. But if the lady decorated the forehead of the knight with roses, then this fragrant ambassador proclaimed: "Your fortune is also mine."

The following tables, giving the significance of flowers in the Orient, in medieval times and in the present day, are here presented as much for the sake of curiosity as for any possible value it may have to eager swains and knowledge-thirsty readers.

The Language of Flowers 173

Significance	Orient	Middle Ages	Present
Aversion		moss-rose	thistle
Departure	rosemary	rosemary	"
Absence	"	"	wormwood
Address	"	broom	"
Doctor	camille	"	"
Distinction	honeysuckle	"	"
Constancy	"	thyme	mistle
Firmness	white rose	"	tea-rose
Visit	jasmine	"	"
Wickedness	"	"	ebony
Brother	cowslip	"	"
Humility	daisy	"	"
Nobility	"	red rose	orange blossom
Jealousy	"	"	stinging nettle
Remembrance	white poppy	pansy	forget-me-not
Encouragement	"	thyme	evergreen
Obedience	"	"	white carnation
Joy	anemone	"	"
Friend	hyacinthe	"	"
Friendship	"	glycine	myrtle
Fear	mint	"	Peruvian marvel
Garden	jasmine	"	"
Wife	myrtle	"	"
Patience	camille	blue violet	"
Prison	poppy	poppy	"
Mystery	"	province rose	maidenhair
Yesterday	violet gillyflower	"	"
Belief	"	lily	"
Happiness	violet gillyflower	"	acacia rose
Grief	"	hyssop	"
Goodness	mayflower	marjoram	potato-plant
Hatred	"	"	basilicum
Anxiety	"	red rosebud	"
Today	red gillyflower	"	"
Hope	savory	white violet	thorn
I	narcissus	"	"
Youth	"	"	white lilac
Wisdom	"	"	marigold
Boldness	beechnut	"	aspen
Sorrow	basilicum	"	"
Vice	"	"	darnelle
Love	"	"	ivy
" approval of	"	white rose	"
" eternality of ivy	"	white gillyflower	ash
" modest	white gillyflower	rosemary	acacia

Significance	Orient	Middle Ages	Present
Love: bands of	white gillyflower	rosemary	honeysuckle
" declaration of	daisy	white rosebud	jonquil
" worthiness of	"	"	jasmine
" storms of	"	thistle	Peruvian marvel
Lies	"	Great marjoram	"
Girl	rose	"	"
Man	carnation	"	"
Melancholy	"	"	willow leaf
Tomorrow	white gillyflower	"	sword-lily
Night	poppy	lettuce	"
Ecstasy	"	"	grapevine
Purity	poppy	"	lily
Trip	larkspur	"	"
Shame	geranium	"	peony
Ship	basilicum	"	,
Pain	red gillyflower	cayenne flower	"
Beauty	"	red gillyflower	wallow
Quiet	buttercup	"	white rose
Soldier	"	"	"
Walk	cress	"	"
Day	daisy	"	"
Dear	reseda	"	"
Tears	rosemary	"	willow leaf
Death	primel	"	"
Fidelity	carnation	"	white rose
Trust	"	"	snowflower
Virtue	"	"	lavender
Ingratitude	ivy	ivy	"
Injustice	"	"	hcps
Uneasiness	"	"	cock's head
Innocence	mayflower	"	"
Infidelity	yellow rose	"	"
Country	violet	"	"
Past	violet gillyflower	"	"
Forsake	"	"	anemone
Treason	stinging nettle	stinging nettle	hemlock
Despair	cypress	"	cypress
Superior	tuberose	"	"
Chief	sunflower	"	"
Refusal	"	moss-rose	"
Widow	pansy	"	scabiosa
Goodwill	"	"	hyacinthe
Pleasure	"	violet	tuberose
Time, lost	"	"	"
Future	white gillyflower	"	"

§ 2

THE FLOWER-CLOCK
FOR
RENDEZVOUS OF LOVERS

Besides their peculiar language, flowers possess still another property of imparting information to the lovers of the time of the rendezvous, according to the hour at which the flower usually opens.

This flower-clock reads:

NAME	TIME
Snowthistle	1 a.m.
Goat's Beard	2 a.m.
Picris	3 a.m.
Barrbinde	4 a.m.
Creeping Ivy	5 a.m.
Scorzonera	6 a.m.
Water-rose	7 a.m.
Red pimper	8 a.m.
Marigold	9 a.m.
Fig	10 a.m.
Star of Bethlehem	11 a.m.
Ice-plant*	12 a.m.
Carnation	1 p.m.
Crepis	2 p.m.
Lion's tooth	3 p.m.
Alysse	4 p.m.
Peruvian marvel	5 p.m.
Geranium	6 p.m.
Lily	7 p.m.
Bindweed	8 p.m.
Nyctanthus	9 p.m.
Purple bindweed	10 p.m.
Silene	11 p.m.
Cactus	12 p.m.

*Misembrianthimum chrystalline

But since all "flower-clocks" do not run on standard time, we complete the above Father Time with a short list of flowers which open and close pretty regularly about the same time in most parts of the world:

NAME	TIME
Matricaria	4 a.m.
Poppy	5 a.m.
Blue and rose bindweed	6 a.m.
Thistle	7 a.m.
Water-rose (in quiet waters)	7 a.m.
Venus-mirror	8 a.m.
Nolana	9 a.m.
Marigold	10 a.m.
Pursilene	11 a.m.
Ficoide	12 a.m.
Silene	5 p.m.
Peruvian marvel	6 p.m.
High-taper	7 p.m.
Purple bindweed	10 p.m.

§ 3

Plants and Flowers of Love
Pumpkins and Pomegranates
in
The Cult of Venus

The ancients consecrated plants and flowers to their divinities, and especially to the love deities. The Orphic Hymns tell us that aromatica is the perfume of nymphs and of Pan; heliotrope is the perfume of Helios-Apollo; myrtle the perfume of the Selenes; verbena the perfume of Artemis; myrrh the perfume of Aphrodite; poppy the perfume of the Nyx; rosemary the perfume of the Nereides; the anemone and the rose, the perfumes of

Adonis; and the Asphodel, the perfume of the Erynnians.

Pumpkins and pomegranates had an important place in the cult of Adonis; the poetess Praxilla highly recommends them to lovers as the fruits preferred by Adonis and which he requires in his ceremonies.

As far as the plants of Venus go, Papus states that they are distinguished by their aroma, like verbena, baldrian, and capillum Veneris; the fruits consecrated to this plant are very sweet, like the pear, fig and orange.

But the rose is the queen of the flowers to lovers. It, alone, is consecrated to Venus and her rites. The Egyptians held it to be the symbol of perfection and in Greek mythology it represented beauty. Opened and fully developed, this flower represents the reflection of woman in the fullness of her charms. As a closed flower, or bud, it denotes the young maiden who has not yet attained the complete beauty and perfection of her sex. Anacreon calls the rose the "honor and magic of the flowers, the pleasure and care of the Spring, the delight of the gods."

§ 4

The Language of Stamps

Hidden Code of Lovers

In order to logically complete the account of the language of the flowers, gems, and the thousand and one means which lovers have found in all ages to enable them to correspond with one another in secret, we would like briefly to mention some of the stratagems connected with the language of "stamps."

The value of the stamp, its coloring, the way it is pasted to the letter, right or left, above or below, straight or upside down, all convey secret information to the lovers and only to those aware of the code. A pale grey three-cent stamp of Washington may thus signify a meeting at three in the morning under the orchard tree, while a brown-shaded one-and-a-half cent stamp of Lincoln may proclaim that the meeting place has been discovered and must be changed. Thus a casual look at the envelope suffices to inform the lover of all her hopes and fears, without the necessity of opening the letter and perhaps betraying its contents to some duenna or chaperon. That this means is a favorable one can be attested by the reader's local postman who daily comes upon dozens of letters whose stamps are apparently of the wrong denomination and which seem to have been affixed to the envelope haphazardly.

This custom is perhaps less poetical than that of the *selam* of the Orient which is a letter consisting of flowers giving the hour of the assignation, etc., by the secret flower language. But at any rate our custom is certainly more practical.

§ 5

THE SCIENCE OF AUGURIES AND PREMONITIONS

"At every step," says Papus, "man attracts or repels the fluids which intersect incessantly in the creative plan of nature. The powers of destiny actually carry on their play without the slightest worry or premonition of the great majority. The dark premonitions and the secret voices of the infinite usually excite only the poets and women subjected to the despotism of the all mighty eros."

The ancients did not fail to impart great weight to divination and the fateful forebodings.

In China prophecy took place by the *piri*, i.e., by inspection of the tortoise: it was burnt alive and the different figures arising from the tremendous heat were carefuly inspected to foretell the future. The *shi* was also frequently used for this purpose. Th *shi* was a peculiar plant which was "consulted with the aid of the famous book of Y-King. If the tortoise and the *shi* are unfavorable to the undertaking of man, then it is only sensible for man to follow its advice and discard the plan, otherwise great misfortune will surely arise," declares the *shi* King.

The immense importance of the auguries in Rome

cannot be imagined by the modern reader. Practically all undertakings were preceded by sacrifices to the gods so that an augury as to the success or failure of the mission, be it commercial or amorous, might be received. As a matter of fact, no love affair was entered upon, or completed without testing in some manner the success or failure of the amour by means of divine auguries. Practically all the Greek and Roman poets who sang of love, mention these love-signs and tokens in their immortal works.

§ 6

The Science of Prophesying

A Myriad Branches

Even today fortune-telling, especially in connection with love affairs and problems, is as popular as ever. It seems as if the gypsy soothsayers will ever be with us. For they evidently fulfill a real need in human society to have been enabled to exist in that profession for so many centuries.

The number of branches of the science of prophecy will be amazing to any but an initiate. We here append only the more important ones:

Aeromancy: The science of prophesying from the phenomena of the air.

The Science of Prophesying

Alectoromancy: The science of prophesying from the letters of the alphabet.

Alomancy: The science of prophesying from salt.

Anthropomancy: The science of prophesying from the entrails of vivisected men and women.

Arithmomancy: The science of prophesying from the properties of numbers.

Astragalomancy: The science of prophesying from dice and leters.

Axinomancy: The science of prophesying from the glowing-hot axes.

Belomancy: The science of prophesying from arrows.

Brizomancy: The science of prophesying from dreams.

Capnomancy: The science of prophesying from sacrificial odors.

Cartomancy: The science of prophesying from cards.

Cephalomancy: The science of prophesying from the formation of skulls.

Ceromancy: The science of prophesying from melted wax.

Chiromancy: The science of prophesying from hands.

Chrithomancy: The science of prophesying from barley.

Cleidomancy: The science of prophesying from keys.

Crommyomancy: The science of prophesying from onions.

Crystalomancy: The science of prophesying from crystal balls.

Dactylomancy: The science of prophesying from rings.

Daphnomancy: The science of prophesying from bayberries.

Enoptropomancy: The science of prophesying from mirrors.

Gastromancy: The science of prophesying from stomach action.

Geloscopy: The science of prophesying from laughter.

Geomancy: The science of prophesying from earth.

Hippomancy: The science of prophesying from the neighing of horses.

Hydromancy: The science of prophesying from water.

Ichthyomancy: The science of prophesying from fishes.

Lampadomancy: The science of prophesying from light.

Lecanomancy: The science of prophesying from gems in water.

Libanomancy: The science of prophesying from sacred incense.

Lithomancy: The science of prophesying from stones.

Margaritomancy: The science of prophesying from pearls.

Myomancy: The science of prophesying from mice and rats.

Oculomancy: The science of prophesying from eyes.

Oenomancy: The science of prophesying from wine.

The Science of Prophesying

Oniromancy: The science of prophesying from nightmares.

Onychomancy: The science of prophesying from finger nails.

Ooscopy: The science of prophesying from eggs.

Ophiomancy: The science of prophesying from snakes.

Ornithomancy: The science of prophesying from birds.

Parthenomancy: The science of prophesying from virginities.

Patmoscopy: The science of prophesying from heartbeats.

Pegomancy: The science of prophesying from springs.

Pyromancy: The science of prophesying from fires.

Rhabdomancy: The science of prophesying from rods.

Rhapsodomancy: The science of prophesying from random verses.

Sciamancy: The science of prophesying from the dead.

Spodomancy: The science of prophesying from ashes.

Sternomancy: The science of prophesying from breasts.

Stolesomancy: The science of prophesying from clothing.

Theomancy: The science of prophesying from the Cabala.

Xylomancy: The science of prophesying from wood.

And these are but the most popular forms of fortune-telling throughout the ages! A complete list of the names alone of all the means employed to prophesy the future would require a good sized volume by itself! Indeed we have not mentioned some of the very popular forms of modern times, such as prophesying from coffee-grounds or tea-leaves. Some of the signs and their meanings in this branch are as follows: a bouquet of four leaves is a certain indication of good fortune; a number of cross-formations indicates success in love; a circle signifies children; a circle with five dots indicates life-long potency, and similar kinds of gratuitous prophecies.

Other methods, such as physiognomy, metascopy (mind-reading), and phrenology, are too popular and have too general a significance for the field of sex and love to deserve any special attention in this work.

§ 7

DAYS FAVORABLE TO FERTILITY IN WOMEN

The ancients laid great stress on the influence that the paths of the planets exerted on our lives. In a calendar dating from the time of the dynasties of Rameses, there are contained rules to observe if misfortune is to be avoided. Strict orders are given not to approach women on the 7th and 17th day of the month Tobi, for coition will prove unfruitful, the male will become impotent and the female sterile. No reasons are given.

Hesiod held that certain days were favorable to love and that some were exceptionally unfavorable. "On the 4th day it is fitting for a bride to be taken into her new home, but avoid the 5th day for the assumption of the new duties, since this will prove dangerous and horrible. It is on that day that the Erynnians ransack the earth to uncover and devastate such unfortunates. The 19th day of the month is the best time for coition and issue."

§ 8

The Planet Venus
Sexual Side of Astrology

The Venus star is the one that is especially valuable to lovers the world over.

> "*Étoile radieuse*
> *Qui te penches vers nous,*
> *Beauté mystérieuse*
> *Dont les yeaux sont si doux!*
> *Du haut du ciel splendide*
> *Sur notre obscure séjour*
> *Verse un rayon limpide,*
> *Verse un rayon d'amour!*"

What poet has not sung of "this pale pearl enfastened in the tent of heaven."

The Seven Spirits of the Planets ascribe the genie Hagith and Raphael to the embassy of Venus: these spirits preside over love and rule over women. They engage the friendship of queens, princesses, and great ladies and through them one can obtain all that one desires. They are to be invoked just before sunrise. Hagith, in particular is the *spiritus familiaris* of Venus.

According to Agrippa's *Occulta Philosophia*, the genii of Venus appear when invoked in a beautiful body of average height; their countenance is pleasant and enchanting; their color is golden; their walk is that of a very pale star; their symbol: beyond the circle a group of young maidens are sporting with one another and are trying to entice the invokers to join them in their merry play; especial representations: a king with a sceptre riding on a camel; a richly clad virgin; a nude virgin; a white and green cloak; green flowers; the *junieprus sabina*.

"Those born under the influence of Venus," says Ely Starr, "love elegant fashions and pale clothes. They crave all sorts of delights without ever being sated or satisfied.

"Their astral signature lends them grace, goodness, tenderness, and pride; friendliness and naïveté.

"Perfumes and flowers are strict necessities to these subjects of Venus. In music they prefer the melody and harmony.

"They like to sing and be applauded, not so much for the purpose of pleasing as for appearing glamorous.

Sexual Side of Astrology

They take great care of their person. They hate unrest, alarm and trouble. Like those influenced by Jupiter they have a good, even disposition."

These are the qualities which the planetary influence has manifested upon them from its good side. Let us now see the reverse side of the medallion.

"If the planet's influence is excessive and occasions transgressions, then it makes a beast of man and gives him low, coarse passions. The eyebrows become bushy and horrible; the nostrils become greatly distended and hirsute: there soon arises in the person's mind a love for all sorts of bizarre and perverse tastes, especially in the field of love."

We can deal but briefly with horoscopy since its elements are well known, and a complete exposition of the science is far from the purposes of this work. It was the universal belief of the ancients that the "planets and stars know our fates and desires." From this belief it was but a step to the notion that if the course of the constellations were planned, a clue to the future would be discovered. It was a common matter in former times for an astrologer to be called in immediately after the birth of a child so that a horoscope might be cast, and its future foretold.

From the sexual side many astrologers claimed that they could read the origin of incestuous sins and sensual love from the stars. Indeed one claimed that syphilis arose in the year 1483 because in the month October of that year, four planets: Jupiter, Mars, the Sun and Mercury were in conjunction and under the fateful sign of disease. It is at least true that about that time syphilis spread to its present-day ravages.

It is perhaps unnecessary to mention that April has always been a favorite month for lovers. The month of June although popularly believed to be the real favorite, should yield its position to April according to recent scientific investigations. It has been found that most births take place in December as a general rule; this of course means that the initial copulations took place during April; hence the superiority and influence of the planet Venus is proven.

CHAPTER TWELVE
DREAMS AND SEXUAL MAGIC

§ 1

Pleasures in Dreams

IN *Die Meistersingerin von Nürnberg,* in connection with the dream of Walter who saw in his sleep a wondrously beautiful Eve who invited him to pluck the forbidden fruit, Wagner has Hans Sachs declaim the following words:

> "*Mein Freund, das grad' ist Dichters Werk,
> dass er sein Traeumen deut' und merk'.
> Glaubt mir, des Menschen wahrster Wahn
> wird ihm im Traume aufgethan:
> all' Dichtkunst und Poeterei
> Ist nichts als Wahrtraum-Deuterei.
> Was gilts, es gab der Traum euch ein,
> wie heut' ihr sollet Sieger sein?*"

Petit-Radet declares that if the length of the dream lasts a whole night long and if there are no interruptions during its course, then it becomes a very moot point whether the reality or the illusion does more to serve our happiness. One is justified in asking who the more fortunate being might be: the sultan who tastes the fruits and pleasures of his seraglio during the daytime but at night is visited by the most dreadful dreams, or the most wretched of his slaves, oppressed during the day with blows and torments but spending his nights in the company of the most enchanting houris in his nocturnal paradise.

§ 2

JOYS OF LOVE IN DREAMS

HASHISH

Pierre Darblay observes in his *Physiology of Love* that passionate dreams form one of the most significant rôles in the chapter of sensual appetites. According to the laws that combine the spirit with the body, the senses, even when they are chained during sleep, remain under the influence of ideas with which they are busied during the day. Who is unable to dream of the object of his love and passion and to form his dream-picture after an apparent reality? And to what debaucheries does the mad phantasy fail to succumb! For there exists therein another law of this union of mind and body: without disturbing the other senses, or, to avoid any ambiguity, without receiving the faculty of imagination from external impressions, the mind possesses the power of carrying out in sleep those desires which are suggested to it by the ideas that employ the will. Under the magic of this erotic impulse the soul possesses the power of transforming into reality by busying its thoughts only in connection with the joys of love.

Sauvages has told the story of a young girl who was often found in a sitting position, insensible to questions and proddings, her arms crossed in front of her bosom, and continually crying out the words: "Jean! Jean! Je demande le Paradis!"

Another young maiden, it is reported by Franck, suddenly let loose a cry as if she had seen a greatly desired object. Although homely to the extreme, her face took on an angelic expression: sitting on her bed, her eyes open and staring heavenwards, her arms outstretched, she cried with heaving breasts: "Oh holy Ludwig, thou most handsome of all, come to me and conceive in me!"

Immerman reports of a lady who suddenly broke off her conversation, fell into ecstasy and appeared to be tasting the imaginary kisses of a mystic lover.

Dr. Max Simon established the fact that hashish produces visions of a number of young maidens of exceptional beauty and that such visions were the product of hallucination, or more frequently, an illusion, without the sensual appetites seeming to be more than usually excited.

Théophile Gautier supports the last proposition in his *Club des Hachichins*, in which the writer relates his own impressions: "With a tranquil, though enchanted, expression I gazed at this garland of beautiful women which crowned the frieze with their divine nudity: I saw perfect shoulders swaying, silvery breasts gleaming, diminutive feet and luxurious hips moving in the most beauteous of curves, without feeling the slightest temptations. The charming ghosts that had so addled St. Anthony made no erotic impressions on me."

We end with the account of a young Egyptian who had only a medium fortune and was passionately enamoured of Archidice, one of the most notorious of Egyptian courtesans. He offered her all his possessions for but a single night with her. Archidice disdainfully spurned his offer. Our lover fled to Venus in his despair and begged her to grant him the favor of possessing the beauty in dream since she had refused him the reality. His prayer was heard but when the avaricious courtesan found out to what extreme he had gone, she had him hailed before the court and demanded payment for this passionate dream. The judges however, bade the beauty to seek payment from the same goddess in her dreams and to acquire in this manner the fictitious gold for the fictitious copulation of her fictitious lover.

§ 3

METHODS OF INTERPRETATION OF DREAMS
ORIENTAL SYSTEMS
FREUDIAN SEX INTERPRETATIONS

The problem of the interpretation of dreams according to definite scientific rules and also by inferring from the contents of the dreams its relation to the life of the dreamer, has been a favorite one in the life of man. Every civilization has had its own method of interpreta-

Methods of Interpretation of Dreams

tion, and each civilization acclaims its own as the most logical method. Our own times, in its frenzied enthusiasm for the method of Dr. Freud, seems to have overlooked the excellent systems contained in the most ancient religious works of the Orientals, of the Zend Avesta, the ancient scripta of the Sabines, of the old and new testaments; in short, wherever there were savants and priests, the importance of dreams as portentous omens of the fates of individuals and nations, was recognized.

Among the Chaldeans, ancient Egyptians, and Assyrians, the interpretation of dreams belonged to the secret science; the Koran contains a great number of such explanations of dreams; the Arabians have an especial codex on this art, a quarto volume of more than a thousand pages.

But all pale into insignificance in contrast with the Freudian analysis of dreams, which has an answer to every dream-problem based almost entirely on sex. A complete account of his method has been given by Dr. Freud himself, in his momentous *Traumdeutung*, but a short account of the sexual processes of the dream will not here prove amiss since it is ordinarily too technical and confusing for the layman. The dream and its psychological analysis forms the basic principle of psychoanalysis in general, but space does not permit an account of the latter within the confines of this work.

Freud sees in the dream, the remainder of the conscious mind in sleep, a reaction to excitations; these are for a small part external, for the most part of a somato-psychic kind. A good deal of the content is related to daily life. Freud here points to the analogy between these dreams and the daydreams of puberty. He further shows that these dreams are very quickly forgotten after awakening, so that repressive tendency must be present. This is the kernel of Freud's conception: The dream is a function of the unconscious. The interpretation of dreams consists in deducing the latent dream-thoughts of the unconscious from the manifest content of the dream, which is a delineation of the above and represents wish-fulfillments, the heart of Freud's theory. These unfilled wishes are founded on primal sexuality and are the disturbing sources of sleep, expressing themselves sometimes in simple sexual symbolism and sometimes in very complex erotic formations. Even the most innocuous seeming dreams are permeated with sexual symbolism according to Freud. A few examples of his method will make the above clear.

§ 4

FREUDIAN CASES

"Two professors of the university who are known to the dreamer are treating him. One of them does something with his penis; he fears an operation. The other

Freudian Cases

one thrusts an iron bar at his mouth so that he loses two teeth. He is bound with four silken cloths."

The sexual significance of this dream can hardly be doubted. The silken cloths are equivalent to an identification with a homosexual of his acquaintance. The dreamer who has never achieved coition, but who has never actually sought sexual intercourse with men, conceives sexual intercourse after the model of the masturbation which he was taught during puberty.

On the other hand, dreams which appear conspicuously innocent usually embody coarse erotic wishes, and we might confirm this by means of numerous examples. But many dreams which appear indifferent and which would never be suspected of any particular significance, can be traced back after analysis, to unmistakable sexual wish-feelings, which are often of an unexpected nature. For example, who would suspect a sexual wish in the following dream until the interpretation had been worked out? The dreamer relates: "Between two stately palaces stands a little house, receding somewhat, and whose doors are closed. My wife leads me a little way along the street up to the little house, and pushes in the door, and then I slip quickly and easily into the interior of a courtyard that slants obliquely upwards."

Anyone who has had experience in the translating of dreams will, of course, immediately perceive that penetrating into narrow spaces, and opening locked doors belong to the commonest sexual symbolism, and will easily find in this dream a representation of attempted coition from behind (between the two stately buttocks of the female body). The narrow slanting passage is of course the vagina; the assistance attributed to the wife of the dreamer requires the interpretation that in reality it is only consideration for the wife which is responsible for the detention from such an attempt. Moreover inquiry shows that on the previous day a young girl who had pleased him entered the dreamer's household. Moreover she had given him the impression that she would not be altogether opposed to an approach of this sort.

§ 5

SEXUAL SYMBOLISM IN DREAMS

When one has become familiar with the abundant use of symbolism for the representation of sexual material in dreams, one naturally raises the question whether there are not many of these symbols which appear once and for all with a firmly established significance, like the signs in stenography. It is extremely tempting to compile a dream book according to the cipher method. Unfortunately, limitations of space allow us to mention here only the most common of sexual symbols that appear in dreams.

All elongated objects, sticks, tree-trunks, and umbrellas (on account of the stretching-up which might be compared to an erection); all elongated and sharp weapons, knives, daggers and pikes are intended to represent the male member. A frequent but not very intelligible symbol for the same is a nail-file (on account of the rubbing and scraping). Little cases, boxes, caskets, closets and stoves correspond to the female part. The dream of walking through a row of rooms is a brothel or harem dream. Staircases, ladders, and flights of stairs, or climbing on these, either upwards or downwards, are symbolic representations of the sexual act. Smooth walls over which one is climbing, façades of house upon which one is letting oneself down, frequently under great anxiety, correspond to the erect human body and probably repeat in the dream, reminiscences of the upward climbing of little children on their parents. "Smooth" walls are men. Tables and boards are women, perhaps on account of the opposition which does away with the bodily contours. Of articles of dress the woman's hat may frequently be definitely interpreted as the male genital. In dreams of men one often finds the cravat as a symbol of the penis; this indeed is not because cravats hang down long, and are characteristic of the man, but also because one can select them at pleasure, a freedom which is prohibited by nature in the original of the symbol.

The list is interminable. The careful reader, after some practice, will be able to make a similar list from the recurring symbols in his dreams and learn indeed that a broad streak of eroticism is the basic fundament of his outwardly normal being.

§ 6

The Magic Art of Creating Erotic Dreams

The art of creating erotic dreams of all sorts, particularly dreams of love, forms an important branch of sexual magic. In his *Mémoire sur quelques papyrus du Louvre,* Maspéro cites Papyrus No. 3229. This manuscript is a demotic papyrus with Greek transcriptions like those which the earliest Egyptologists called gnostic papyri. The manuscript is unfortunately somewhat damaged and it is impossible to give a complete textual version. It consists of four invocations whose purpose is to send dreams to certain unknown persons.

In the first invocation the nature of the desired dream is directly given: "Come to me in the night and appear in spirit if not in deed, so that you may console me throughout the weary and lonesome hours of the night." The magical recipe is lacking. It is surmised that the ingredients consisted of the lotus leaf, bay, corn, etc.

The next two are both invocations to the god Anubis, but the magical recipes are completely lacking, although the papyrus contains a great many magic names which must be repeated, and a few rites that must be observed.

The Magic Art of Creating Erotic Dreams

There is a more or less complete account of the procedure: "Take a new lamp whose wick is constructed of pure threads of linen, fill it with unmixed oil, light it, write your invocation on a new leaf of papyrus; place it on the tongue of the lamp. Repeat the above-mentioned names four times. The spirit will come to you...."

The above papyrus is sufficient proof that the magic dream art traces an unbroken path from the hoary ages to medieval times and even to our own proud modern scientific century.

In the work *l'Art de se rendre heureux par les songes* there is the following recipe by whose aid the beloved will appear in a dream and grant his favors: "Take two ounces of the roots of convolvus scammonia and dessicated roman camomile; 3 ounces of codfish bones and tortoise; mix this with 5 ounces of fat from a male beaver and with 2 ounces of blue convolvus scammonia. Cook together with 1 ounce of honey and 6 drachmas of dew taken from an opium poppy. Place in a hermetically closed flask. Let it bake in the hot summer sun for two months and let it cool in the cellar in sand throughout the winter. The result will more than pay for the trouble undergone. An application of this salve at night will invariably produce the image of the beloved in dreams, and his actions will be so realistic that the love-partner will actually believe that they are taking place; only awakening will bring disillusion."

In the eighteenth and nineteenth centuries even more ludicrous formulas were laboriously prepared. How many women have thus found solace in creating an image of the absent or unattainable lover in their sleep and having him do everything they desire, to their heart's content, without any embarrassing consequences or questions? Indeed one of the court ladies of Louis XIV, roundly abused her lover for entering her bedchamber at night when she lay dreaming of him: she preferred a figment of the mind to the reality!

The effect, of course, of all these formulas is only psychologic, although the ingredients were usually of so unpalatable a nature that they at any rate caused the person to dream! but it could not guarantee the nature of the dream: the girl could just as easily have been embraced by an old, pock-marked libertine as a fair young Casanova; the man might just as easily have had to flee the embraces of a haggard old maid as to dream of lying comfortably in his fair friend's embraces.

CHAPTER THIRTEEN

SEXUAL MUSIC AND DANCES

§ 1

Sexual Influence of Music
The Food of Love
Demetrius Polyorketes' Mad Love for Lamia

"Music," a philosopher of the Pythaforean school has said, "is the art of exciting by tonal combinations those intelligent men gifted with specially trained organs." Bellaigue recalls in his *Psychologie musicale* the phrase of Shakespeare: "Music is the food of love"; as well as the cry of Musset: "Langue que pour l'amour inventa le génie!"

"With less poesy and more spirit," says the learned commentator, "Berlioz has remarked that while love can give no conception of music, the latter, on the other hand, can give a very definite conception of love! Indeed, not only does it give an idea of love, but even love-ideas; music expresses and influences love."

More than one singer has had to thank her most fortunate conquests to the magic of her voice. One of the strangest of incidents in this connection is the love of Demetrius Polyorketes, King of Macedonia, for the courtesan Lamia, the daughter of a certain Cleanor of Athens. As a result of a sea-battle near one of the islands of Cypris, Lamia fell into the hands of Polyorketes. She was at least forty years old. Although a courtesan and flutist it appears that she was true to Demetrius. Plutarch quotes the following letter which she wrote to her royal lover: "Indeed, since this divine night I have done nothing that might make me unworthy of your goodness, although you have allowed me unlimited power of satisfying my desires. But my conduct is irreproachable; I have allowed myself no liaisons. I do not treat you like the hetæræ, I do not deceive you, my king, as the others do. Nay! By Venus Artemis! since that time neither oral nor written advances have been made me, for you are feared and regarded as unconquerable." Demetrius preferred Lamia to his other far younger and handsomer mistresses Leäna, Chrysis, Antipyra and Demo.

Machon who cites Athenæus, introduces us to some of the secret love adventures of this old flutist. He expressly states that Demetrius still imagined he was in the bed of his mistress, heard her playing and was seized by the joy of the rhythm. He adds that of all the pleasant perfumes that Asia knew how to extract from plants, no perfume was so pleasant to Demetrius as the impure perspiration of the body of Lamia "who rubbed her pudendum with her hand and had carnal intercourse with her fingers." Lamia would forget in her love frenzy that she was copulating with a king and would hold him fast and gasping with her prolonged love-maddened bites.

One day Demetrius feigned to prefer Leäna to her.

But Lamia threw her arms around his neck and softly drew him to her bed while she whispered to him: "Certainly! You shall also have Leäna if you desire it." The name *leainan*, in the erotic language, signified one of the mysteries of the hetæra profession, and Lamia, in speaking of her colleague, meant only a lustful position in coition. Thus the love of Demetrius for this old magician knew no bounds. Many coarse jokes were naturally made of the affair without the slightest effect on either. The King of Macedonia asserted that if he granted that Lamia was no longer young, the goddess Venus was still older and was not worshipped a whit less because of this. He became irreconcilably antagonized to the Thracian king, who had jested of his love for Lamia. Demetrius declared that his "whore" was more modest than Penelope, the wife of Lysimachus, the Thracian king.

Lamia is also said to have thus answered the judgment of the court on the already cited case of Archidice who was told to look for her "whore-fee" in her dreams: "I find this unjust, for the shadow of the gold does not quiet the desires of Archidice, while the dream satifies the passion of her lover."

At her death the Athenians proclaimed her a goddess and erected a temple to her under the name of Venus-Lamia.

§ 2

SEX PERMEATES MUSIC OF GOUNOD
SEXUAL EXALTATION IN WAGNER'S MUSIC
TRIUMPHANT EROTIC MUSIC OF BERLIOZ
PERVERSIONS AND MUSIC

There are a great number of famous works of music which are pure pages of sex. To this category belong: the serenade in *Don Juan*, the delightful, sensual song of the cherubim in the *Marriage of Figaro*, the great duet in the *Hugenottes*, the verses in Gounod's *Sappho*, the farewell scene in *Romeo and Juliet*, the garden scene in *Faust*, of which Bellaigue says: "It is sex that Gounod sings of, pure and simple. Between Faust and Margaret appear no intermediary thoughts, no expressions of fear and the like. It is simply that they love each other and give themselves to their love, without any restraint. Even the flower replies that she must love in answer to her query."

Gounod has indeed attained much for love, if it has not returned as much for him. Sex permeates almost all his work and indeed his entire temperament seems to be devoted to the task of making his feelings felt in music.

In Richard Wagner's *Tristan and Isolde*, occultism comes to the fore and explains the eternal tragedy of love. To the learned eye of the initiate all the objects, all the external properties, contain a symbolic signifi-

Triumphant Erotic Music of Berlioz

cance and became highly erotic incidents. His immense *Tannhäuser* is no less a sexually exciting work in his contradistinction between the passionate pagan sex and the Christian, legal love. Indeed lovers of Wagnerian music confess to a sexual exaltation which appears but rarely in the works of other composers. Inasmuch as Wagner intended his opera to be a perfect combination of music and drama it would require too technical a description here in explanation of its manifold eroticism. The reader is advised to closely analyze his sensations at the next Wagnerian recital he attends and to examine for himself the sexual fundament of the associations aroused in him by the music.

Berlioz's *Symphonie fantastique* represents perhaps the climax of sexual music. Conceived under the influence of a great passion, Berlioz attempted to describe the tormenting fires of love that swept his inner being. All thoughts, ideas and expressions are interpreted from the standpoint of sex. Since the story of this astounding work may not be as familiar to the modern reader as the Wagnerian operas, we recount it in some detail.

A young poet wishes to commit suicide. The cause? Love, of course. He swallows a narcotic. The dose however is too weak and instead of killing him it creates the most peculiar hallucinations. He dreams that he has killed the person whom he loves, and the memory of his victim weighs upon him: They are dancing to the tunes of a waltz, accompanied by a primitive orchestra. It is this waltz that makes everything so confusing. The waltz sings, enchants, triumphs. It heats the blood until the head whirls about in maddened frenzy. This waltz is no common *leit-motif*: it is the corporeal lover, it is the fleshly act, it is sex in all its glory triumphant, dazzling the eyes of the lovers until they become sex-mad with dance and are forced to yield to their desires.

But this musical coition is not completed: the scene suddenly changes; a storm breaks out; all becomes black.

The approach to the execution. The hour of death has arrived. In the midst of a dusky accompaniment, in which the sorrowful tones of a march echo the relentless, dull rhythm, he walks to his death. The last moment has come; sword, ax, knife, retaliation is to fall on his bare and trembling body.... And there, there it is again, that maddening waltz, swaying over the crashing harmony of the brass instruments. As the fatal stroke starts to fall, the soul escapes with the release of the orchestra.

But again the scene changes. It is midnight. Slow intonations of bells call magicians and witches to the sabbath, which is played with all the erotic, satanic customs. In order to honorably receive the soul of the poet, the devil's assembly celebrates a parody of the mass of the dead, and the *Dies Iræ* comes forth, caricatured, grotesque, sarcastic. As the end of the mass begins the hellish roundelay of sin, accompanied by the clash of the brass instruments and the stormy passions of that waltz he had danced with his sweetheart, and which never leaves his mind, follows him into all eternity.

It is but a step from the passionate music of Berlioz to the logical outcome of his love-waltz: copulation to the tune of some pertinent music! Two works have proved to be very popular with the class of perverted persons who go in for this sort of new sexual thrill. If the couple prefers a fast, spirited beat, the Cummunist rallying song, *Internationale*, is used; but if they feel the need of a slow measured beat, the inspiring tunes of Handel's *Largo* are used; Indeed erotic verses have been written to both of the above works so that the couple can sing if they so desire during coition! Or, what the ancient black magic would have considered the blackest of black magic, phonographs can grind out the music which has been perverted to such ends, for special records of the above works are sold in secret by dealers who pander to such lascivious tastes.

§ 3

SEXUAL DANCES SEDUCTION OF THE COURTESANS
EROTIC DANCES

We close our slight excursus into the realm of æsthetics, which relates to our subject only insofar as it calls upon the same sensual appetites, with a slight discussion of the sexual element in dances.

Indeed the two are so closely related that the sermons on the immorality of dances by Christian clergymen are too common and well known for us to quote them; we would rather give a short description of some of the most famous of sexual dances: the dance of the bayadere, the stomach dance, the tarantella, the flamanda and the czardas.

The *Ramayana* describes the means used by the courtesans to seduce the anchorite: They suddenly appear to the guest, surround him as if he were the central figure of a chorus and seem to make their every movement proceed from his vicinity. Lascivious gestures employing every part of the body are usually sufficient to cause the man to seize one of the girls and to retire with her to the privacy of a booth. But if the gestures fail, then the courtsans resort to their crowning stroke. They encircle him, bend their heads backwards till they reach the floor, then, with protruding stomachs they shake their hips so violently that the thin girdles fall to the floor and before the startled eyes of the spectator there seems to be nothing but a circle of black, sexual triangles! No man, the guide told us, has ever remained unmoved in face of such an astounding sight.

In order to appreciate the immense influence of the dance on the sexual sense, one must go to Biskra where the daughters of the Ouled-Naïl dance at evening. We first step into a local café and are certain to find there a young Turkish girl of brown skin. Her great black eyes

Seduction of the Courtesans

sparkle. The *souak* has painted her teeth red, her gums and lips a deep purple. Arms and legs are bare, but they have been completely hennaed until the finger and toe nails gleam like the fruits of the ju-jube tree. The forehead, nose, chin and cheeks are covered with little blue stars tattooed into the skin. A girdle of silver covers the privates.

First she assumes some passionate and provocative attitudes as a prelude to the corporeal act, which she now begins to represent. It is the invitation to the lover, an invitation full of erotic promises, for she has thrown her head back, and with an expiring expression, outstretched bosom, quivering breasts and trembling hips, offers herself. Now the lover comes. She receives him with passionate excitement as if drunk with love. More violent become her movements until the line from her breasts to the hips seems to have become one continuous curve; she is inexhaustible in the art of love-embraces, until finally, her forehead bathed in sweat, she falls to the floor in an actual swoon, exhausted by her passions.

The "belly-dance," whose being is rooted in obscenity, is exceptionally widespread. It is found among the inhabitants of Australia, Polynesia, West Africa, South America and especially in Egypt, Tunis and Algiers. The Kannaki of Hawaii call it the *hula-hula* and in this form it has become very well known by means of the motion picture. What is less known, however, is that the *hula-hula* is a communal affair in which the dancers seek to excite the assembled men by lascivious movements of the hips, until the men become intoxicated with the complicated rhythm and move their own hips frenziedly about. Wild cries and shouts greet this male accompaniment and the assembly pairs off into couples with the naturally resulting sexual consequences. When the male's sensual appetites have once been roused by dance, no will power or morality can keep him from sexually enjoying himself if the opportunity is at hand.

Dr. Wolff noticed the following queer dance among the negroes of the Kuango country in West Africa: "The dance here consists almost entirely of movements of the buttocks. Rows of men stand opposite to rows of women, each buttock touching a buttock; swaying their hips and buttocks they move apart for a little distance, rest awhile, then proceed backwards until the buttocks touch again, when they turn about and embrace one another. They remain in this posture for a while and then begin the entire affair over again. This is the queerest spectacle imaginable, especially if one stands in the very center: all one sees are black buttocks embracing black buttocks!"

In Tunis the *danse du ventre* is danced everywhere, in the lowest dens as well as at private parties and at certain ceremonies. Gaston Vuiller tells of the time he was invited to a Jewish wedding at Tunis. After the orchestra had played a prelude, a maiden with modest downcast eyes entered the room. She slowly lifted her

Erotic Dances

eyelids and threw a languishing glance at the guests. With half-closed eyes she began to dance and to make lascivious movements with her body that contrasted strangely with the solemnity of the preceding religious ceremony. The other women joined the obscene gestures of the dancer with cries of "you-you," a custom peculiar to the stomach dance.

The dance of the Indian bayaderes and the houris of the Orient are quite similar to the tarantella of the Neapolitans, the flamande of the Spanish gitanas, the czardas accompanied by the blood-red glare of the evening sunset: all are passionate, exciting dances, true pantomimes of love, whose frenzy and drunkenness they perfectly express.

In all these sexual dances there can be plainly seen by the terpsichorean connoisseur the elements of an actual coition: The approach of the lover, the offer of the woman's body; the preliminary excitation of the couple, their slow union in copulation, the gradually quickening beat of the male, the answer of the girl, a fast, mad, whirling dance announces the climax; then slow, retreating steps announce the complete satirety and satisfaction of the sexual act in pantomime!

Every dance contains some element of eroticism in it and the reader may afford himself much pleasure by noting in the future more carefully how the sexual basis of the dance is laboriously, if unconsciously, enacted by the dancing couple.

CHAPTER FOURTEEN
CHRISTIANITY AND SEX MAGIC

§ 1

Christianity and Sex
Religious Erotomania

UNDOUBTEDLY the Galilean rabbi was of a modest nature. If he found favors in the society of Martha and Mary, if other young and beautiful women had the tenderest feelings for the master, it is certainly true that the attraction which Jesus drew to himself was free of every fleshly combination. Christianity damned sex and love, held carnal connection to be a monster, and even preached continency in marriage. The theologians quarrelled very seriously over the problem whether marital coition was a sin, since it was only half for the preservation of the species and half for the production of pleasure.

Sylvius, among others, asserts that it is a venial sin to give oneself pleasure by the procreative act; for this pleasure that has its sources in corruption is a shameful thing and is capable of blinding the reason. On the other hand, Dominicus, Sotto, Sanchez, and others assert that it is no sin in the case where it is engaged in for the fructification of the womb. Pope Innocence XI., even damned pleasure in marital coition.

René Louvel, in his *Traité de chasteté* states that coition was only good and seemly insofar as it coincided with the natural reason, and that it was perverse when it was practiced only for the pleasure that it created, since according to the law of nature the former was a consequence of the act and the act not a consequence of nature.

"It is therefore not evil," he says, "when the parents cohabit in order to beget children and experience the pleasure that is connected with the act, excepting that they do not find too much pleasure therein. It is good that certain wives carry their modesty to a degree that finds this pleasant feeling to be blameworthy and are hence less ready to acquiesce to the wishes of their not so devout husbands."

The casuists taught the people how to practice coition so that they would not run the perils of excommunication and damnation.

If the husband, they taught, aroused himself by obscene methods, it was a mortal sin laying him open to the danger of premature ejaculation; but if all this occurred only for the purpose of the marital act, then it was at most a venial sin, always excepting that it did not go beyond a certain seemly and permissible degree. In fact, if an act is permitted then the means for the production of the act should naturally also be permitted. This is also the opinion of St. Anthony, among others. One could not very easily demand a couple to jump immediately to the climax of the sexual act without some intermediate steps.

Dubreyne makes no less subtle distinctions on the

problems of kisses in his *Moechialogy*. He holds that kisses, even those apparently conjugal but grounded in passion, given by persons of different sexes to one another are mortal sins, especially if one lingers happily on the lips. He adds that the kiss from mouth to mouth, especially when accompanied by the introduction of the tongue into the other's mouth must be considered a mortal sin. Such kisses whether given in play or sport or only as proof of friendship, effect considerable influence on sensual excitation and hence are to be strongly condemned. Such is also the opinion of St. Liguori. Similarly kisses on unusual parts of the body, e.g., on the breasts, nipples, etc., are held to be indecent and a great social danger and hence mortal sins.

The denial of a great law of sex has led the churchmen to such anomalous erotic perversions. Yet on the other hand it must be emphasized that many of the precepts of the Catholic moralists must be evaluated as eminently sensible from a medical standpoint.

Catholic moralism condemns unequivocally the application of all means and methods which would hinder conception,—with but one single exception. On the assumption that sexual intercourse will not prove fruitful at certain times, the married couples in France refrain from coition at those times in which they believe conception is possible. This time lies somewhere between the two monthly periods according to experience. It begins fourteen days after the appearance of the last menstruation and ends a few days before the next one.

Conception is more likely to appear three to four days before the appearance of the next menses. This fact has been well known to those desirous of limiting offspring.

The Jesuits claim that this procedure is not in the least contrary to the moral law and the very devout Dr. Capellmann wrote a book entitled *Facultative Sterility without Injury to Moral Law*, which has had a great circulation in Catholic centers as shown by its many translations.

On the other hand the Catholic moralists have condemned as mortal sins those acts of the wife having anything to do with the dislodgment of the semen from its proper resting place: such acts, as arising after the copulation in order to pass water and the semen with it. Today we know that such procedures are entirely useless. The walls of the vagina are contracted immediately after the withdrawal of the man and are so airtight that no release of semen is possible.

Far more interesting and notable are the precepts of the Catholic moralism on other features of normal and legal intercourse. The boldness of their conception is extremely surprising.

Thus we have a problem: "How do you judge the withdrawal of a man after he has spent his seed without making his wife moist?" And the answer according to Scavinii's *Theologia moralis universa*: "It is the general opinion that the woman should be immediately excited from the first contact to the moistening since this belongs to the perfection of the marital act. This is true not because the moistening of the woman is essential but because it aids the possibility of conception, for nothing is done without reason by nature. And from this it is to be deduced that those women who turn their mind to other things than the sexual act so that they shall not be properly impregnated have committed mortal sins; as have those men sinned who have not properly awaited the moistening of the woman."

The moralists however easily saw that is was impossible for the man to wait for the moistening of the woman since immediately after the seminal discharge the masculine member became detumescent. In this case according to Catholic moral theory the women should create the proper satisfaction by contact and manipulation either from the hands of the husband or by herself. Thus for example St. Liguori declares: "All moralists allow women who are of cold nature to excite themselves by contact before marital union so that they will become moist in the resulting copulation."

This is also the opinion of the Jesuit, Gury; marriage gives to both parties the right to satisfy the sexual instinct; if, however, the woman is unable to attain the satisfaction that should normally result from the sexual act and if the fault is not her own, then it should by all means be allowed the woman to properly prepare herself by such embraces and contacts as will tend to enhance the possibility of complete satisfaction.

Unusual postures in coition are also allowed by Catholic moralists or are considered at the worst as venial sins. St. Liguori declares: "Every position in coition, even if it be unnatural (standing, sitting, animal fashion, by the side, or the man taking the passive and nether part) is in itself no more than a venial sin whereby the marital act may be concluded. Change of position does not hinder conception since the semen of the man does not flow into the womb but proceeds there by attraction, the womb attracting the semen to it by natural means."

The Jesuit, Gury, notes: "1. Husbands who change position in the sexual act because of fear of miscarriage during pregnancy, or on account of the corpulency or stature of the man, the tiredness or sexual coldness of a woman, or the desire for greater excitation from unusual postures, are not guilty of committing sins. 2. Any position which is possible, no matter how difficult or fanciful it may appear, must not be decried even if a certain loss of semen results, since but one seed is necessary for the fructification of the womb."

From the medical standpoint, these precepts of Catholic moralism must be highly praised. Modern science has demonstrated that under certain conditions an unusual posture in coition will conquer previous consistent sterility in women. Thus Dr. Kisch advised corpulent men with prominent stomachs to copulate in the side-position, in order to make more certain of impregnation and conception. Casper tells of a case where a very pinguid woman who had been sterile for a long time, conceived after she had been copulated in the stomach-position. In cases where the womb lies very far back and the lips of the vagina protrude very prominently Dr. Kisch advises coition to be performed in an erect sitting posture on the man so that the womb may be placed in the most favorable position for impregnation.

Less excellent though just as liberal and wise are the precepts of Catholic moralism on coition during menstruation and pregnancy.

In order to cure sterility in women, Catholic moralists allow all sorts of means, no matter how indecent they may appear.

In this connection the famous advice of Van Swieten, the physician of the Empress Maria Theresa, is pertinent. Her marriage had proven unfruitful for a long time and at last in desperation the doctor was called in. After a thorough examination he turned to her and said: "All that is necessary is for the vulva of your most holy majesty to be tickled for some time before the actual act of copulation." The physician's advice was followed and was justified nine months later.

All such measures are allowed by the moralists insofar as they serve the actual purposes of marriage.

But on the other hand they hold sexual mutilation, castration, to be sinful. "No year of my practice passes by," says the devout Dr. Stohr, "in which I am not approached by youths and men who desire me to castrate them either on account of their suffering from consistent masturbation or from pollution. This operation is still caried out in this day and age for the above reasons. It is as absolutely unjustified from a moral standpoint as it is objectionable from a scientific standpoint; it always shows lack of strong will and diseased, even desperate, pusillanimity on the part of the patient when he presents this request to the doctor. For many years similar operations on women under similar predispositions (diseases and inflamed sexual instinct) have been made in England. This is the excision of the clitoris, the feminine organ of pleasure. A well-known women's doctor in London, Baker-Brown, who in spite of many warnings against this inadmissible and infamous operation, committed the offense so repeatedly that he was at last expelled from the Royal College of Surgeons."

As the Catholic Church desires no child to die unbaptized it has done much to encourage cæsarean operations. There are numerous cases where priests themselves have undertaken this operation.

The Catholic Church has even made wet-nurses objects of their rules. Thus the Jesuit, Gury, states: "The mother must nourish her children with her own milk since this is obviously desired by natural law. Nevertheless this obligation does not come under that of a mortal sin. Necessity, considerable value or custom in high families, absolves mothers from all blame, but they are responsible for the behavior and health of a good wet-nurse under penalty of heavy sins."

Unfortunately the Catholic Church seeks to enhance

that false modesty of women which is so often shown in attempted physical investigations by physicians. According to the theologists the woman is justified in refusing to disrobe herself before the eyes of the physician even if it is a matter of life or death.

P. de Régla observes "that the church in its attempt to construe the most natural acts in the world as sins and to idealize the material principle of procreation, has shown itself perhaps more erotic in the mystic sense of the word than the pagans who used as a principle of procreation the completely natural symbol of the masculine sexual member. Inasmuch as the church burdened nature in its normal manifestations by threats of excommunication, the result was the spreading of what we call prostitution. The Church has made illegal what is legal and has inundated countries with temples dedicated to Venus Mercenaria where she rules without check and with absolute authority.

"From such attacks the natural ceremonies of the ancients have fled to the darkness of modern lupinarians. That which was a natural and human act has been transformed into a shameful vice from which have arisen all the punishable practices which really form prostitution.

"With its disappearance from public view, phallicism lost its symbolic radiance and became a smeary and disgusting lamp lighting up human shamefulness. The beautiful Venus of the ancients has become a little Madonna, which can still be found at the heads of the ithyphallic places of prostitution in central Italy and Spain.

"No longer do these fallen goddesses beg from Venus and Priapus, fortune, joy and wealth, but from the modern Christian queen of heaven, the Virgin Mary."

Without speaking of the cult of the holy Præputius which completes that of the heathen phallophoria, it is unmistakable to those who knew the inner connection between the erotic and religious feeling that this so ethereal passion for the Virgin, (as she is cherished by so many young priests and even staid theologians) represents an especial discharge of erotomania and that it was the glowing sex that inspired the works of these celibates. They call her the new Eve, the sublimate gateway of mercy through which the Savior has once appeared and through which he will some day come again. She is the supreme happiness, the queen of heaven surrounded by the nine angel choirs, the mother of the beautiful neighborly love, the treasure of God. She is further the source, a splendid armor for the Holy Ghost, a divinity attracting the divine trinity, the city of God, the throne of God, the temple of God, the world of God. They compare her with an earthly paradise created from virgin earth with modest flowers, with rich green pastures of hope, with unstormable towers, and with a rapturous temple of honor.

Zola writes in the *Sins of the Abbé Mouret*: "This misplacement of women in the jealous and cruel heaven of the Old Testament, this white form placed at the feet of the fearsome trinity, represents the grace and mercy of religion itself, a refuge to those lost in the mysteries of the dogmas."

§ 2

THE REACTION
THE EROTICO-RELIGIOUS PERVERSIONS

While Christianity was denouncing sex and love, magic opened its gates wide for their reception; for the redemption was based on the sinful fall of the first man, and this sinful fall was the result of a curious mixture of the devil who from the time of paradise restlessly practiced his corrupt handiwork through all ages. The Bible tells how legions of demons are spread around the world in order to injure the work of God, to change good into bad, to circulate plagues of all kinds, to tempt mankind, to drive them to perversions and crimes, to drag down into the depths of hell the greater half of the human race by their clever machinations.

"For a long time," states Morin, "Christianity has immeasurably strengthened the rôle of the evil spirits and thereby created a rival of God. The Church has further admitted that certain persons, in concluding pacts with demons, are thereby enabled to participate in their power and to pervert the laws of nature by

The Reaction

releasing thunderstorms, spreading draughts upon the fields, influencing their fellow men from a distance and inflicting upon them a mass of evils, even death. These are the magicians whose existence and attributes are confirmed by a mass of canons, by religious monuments and reminiscences of the greatest savants.

In the following chapters we become acquainted with the rôle played by Satan in the ceremonies of the witches' sabbath, in the Black Mass, in the obscene hallucinations of the incubi and succubi.

Christianity preaches continency and modesty to attain this perfection. Desires must be suppressed, the flesh must be mortified and castigated. Thus Christianity became the cause of the most cruel extravaganza from which the erotic factors were not always missing. In fact an undoubtable relationship exists between religion, cruelty and pleasure. "Religious and sexual feelings," says Krafft-Ebing in his *Psychopathia Sexualis*, "show in the height of their development complete agreement in the quantity and torment of excitation and can therefore under certain circumstances act vicariously. Both may be transformed into cruelty under pathologic conditions."

Origenes and Leontius of Antioch had themselves made eunuchs of their own free will. They had many devotees and imitators. Among the latter belong the Scopts who appeared in Russia and spread very rapidly up till the World War.

Under the rule of Catherine II., and Alexander I., the

individuality of their sect was greatly strengthened by castration. In the first period of their existence the operation consisted of the removal of the testes by glowing hot irons; this mutilation was called the baptism by fire. Later the amputation was made more humane by the application of a chisel or a razor after the scrotum had been firmly tied. This mutilation was not, however, the ideal of the Scopts; they named it as follows: The first seal, the little seal, the first white, the first purity, the mounting of the piebald horse. When castration took place on adults, erection was still possible for some time thereafter and the victims did not entirely lose the possibility of sinning. Hence they came upon the idea of also removing the penis, which they called complete baptism, second or imperial seal, mounting of the white horse.

The women who belong to the sect were also horribly mutilated. The nipples of their breasts were either cut, torn or burnt away. At times, a part of the labia minora of the vagina together with the clitoris were cut off, or the upper half of the labia minora and majora completely removed. There is a more or less credible legend of the Scopts in their custom of mutilating a young virgin the night before Easter; from that time on she was considered holy. Her breasts were removed and then the participants in the ceremony awesomely consumed a portion of the holy breasts. The virginal victim was then placed upon the altar; the frenetic believers danced and sang about her until they were aroused to the highest pitch of sexual madness when they gave way to their cruel and bestial desires upon one another.

CHAPTER FIFTEEN

MYSTIC SEXUAL MISCELLANIES

§ 1

ECSTASY AND SEX

So CLOSE is the relationship of ecstasy and sex that Dr. Steingiesser asserts: "Ectasy is apparently always accompanied by sexual excitation, if not by sexual corruption." The enthralling feeling of rapture, the loss of sensation of personality, the thrill of delight and the recedence of the external world are undoubtedly very closely connected with the passionate glow of coition.

Naturally the sexual excitation during ecstasy is best noted in the conduct of the saints, to whom that enraptured state was no particular novelty. Veronica Juliani, who was proclaimed blessed by Pope Pius VII., had herself given in marriage to the Holy Lamb, and even took a little lamb to bed with her and had it suck from her breasts. So great was the excitation aroused in her that the breasts of this virgin saintess actually gave forth a few drops of milk!

St. Armelle, a peasant girl of Bretagne, believed that her spiritual lover had so kindled the fire of love in her heart, that she had become externally and internally but fire and flame. The arrow of her lover, says her pious biographer, a French Ursuline, had wounded her heart so that she looked for him incessantly. (The reader should here compare the notorious group of St. Theresa of Bernin, who sank in hysterical impotence on a marble cloud while her enamoured angel pierced her heart with the arrow of divine love, as proof that the graphic arts were well aware of the close connection).

Jeanne de Cambray and Angelina de Foligny declared that the divine presence had appeared to them and that they had sexual intercourse with him. St. Mechtildis asserted similarly of the deity, but gave more details: "He kissed my hand, pressed me to Him, whispered to me to give Him my love, and I surrendered my all to Him and in return tasted of His divine essence."

Maria Magdalena de Pazzi would often stand fixed in her worship until she felt the throes of psychic sexual delight coming over her. When she finally reached the climax, she would sigh loudly in praise of the Lord, pick up her moistened habit and kneel in front of the altar. St. Catherine of Genoa, in spite of her sainthood, suffered a similar love-passion. When seized by an attack of psychic bliss, she would throw herself to the ground in order to cool herself off and would cry aloud: "Love, love, I can bear such delight no longer!" She also felt especially drawn to her father confessor; once she placed his hand to her nose and inhaled such an odor that it penetrated to her heart. "Such a divine odor," she cried. "would even awaken the dead."

We could go on endlessly with such instances but we think our point has been made clear. The reader curious for more details of the above cases is referred to the learned doctor's *Sexual Life of the Saints*.

We would like, however, to give Jacques de Voragine's account of the martyrdom of St. Paul, the Eremite, as a reverse example of the ecstasy of martyrdom.

The martyr, who was very young, was stretched out on a bed, his hands and feet securely bound. A very beautiful young woman was brought in and she tried to tempt him to sin. He feared he would be unable to resist temptation another moment and hence bit off his tongue and spat it into the face of the temptress: "Thus pain drove out temptation."

§ 2

MAGICAL POWERS OF VIRGINAL PERSPIRATION

SUNAMITISM

ELIXIR FOR LENTHENING MAN'S LIFE

There exists an ancient belief that the physical perspiration of young persons on old ones, especially if they are of opposite sexes, gives to the latter a healthier, longer and more favorable life. But any sexual intercourse is strongly indicted.

The first example of this kind of cure is told in the Bible: "Now King David was old and stricken in years; and they covered him with clothes, but he gat no heat. Wherefore his servants said unto him. Let there be sought for my Lord the king a young virgin: and let her stand before the king, and let her cherish him, and let her lie in his bosom, that my Lord the king may get heat. So they sought for a fair damsel throughout all the coasts of Israel, and found Abishag, a Shunnamite, and brought her to the king. And the damsel was very fair, and cherished the king, and ministered to him: *but the king knew her not.*"

Five hundred years ago there was found an ancient marble monument with the following inscription: "To Aesculapius and Sanitas this is placed by L. Clodius Hermippus who lived 115 years and 5 days by the perspiration of a young virgin, causing great wonder to all the physicians. May posterity lead similar lives in this fashion!"

At any rate the kings and nobles certainly followed his advice! Court memoirs and gossip are full of such tales. Practically every important king and noble from medieval up to modern times had at some time or other essayed this elixir of life. It is a debated subject whether the sunamites remained chaste after the night's embrace.

But sunamitism did not reach its height until the eighteenth century, when it flourished especially in the Palais Royal of Paris. The pimpesses who had their quarters there recruited for this purpose innumerable maidens who had to be in the first blush of their youth and in perfect health. Old men and prematurely impotent young men flocked to the Palais Royal for their services.

Rétif de la Bretonne, the self-appointed biographer of the Palais Royal, devotes an entire volume to the practices of the sunamites. The most famous pander of sunamites was the notorious Madame "Janus," as she is called by Rétif. She kept more than forty girls recruited continually from the provinces, at the disposal of her clients. She very seldom retained a girl who had been born in Paris. As the wife of a physician she was well versed in her craft and served her clients faithfully. Her pupils lived in a house "on the other side of the boulevard" especially built for the needs of the profession. They ate the healthiest of foods and had to take daily physical exercise. Madame Janus took a louis-d'or a night from the oldsters who required the "resurrection." Each girl received six francs, she herself twelve. The first time she herself was present to administer. First the guest was given an aromatic bath, then massaged and dried until his body was completely cleansed. Then a heavy muzzle (muselière) was placed on him and he was laid to bed with two sunamites so that their skins would be in close contact with his.

Two virgins would serve him in this manner for only eight nights when they were replaced by a fresh pair. The first pair then took baths, refreshed themselves and rested for fourteen days when they were again brought into service, for three couples of virgins were necessary for one man.

Great heed was taken to see that the sunamites remained virgins, for loss of virginity would work greater danger on the patient, financially as well as physically. Indeed if the patient wrought a miracle he would have to pay heavy damages to the seduced virgin; as a precaution a large sum of money was placed on deposit with the matron before the "cure" was undertaken. A girl lasted only three years, counting from the time she attained puberty. If the girl were used every day she was good for only one year. To increase the aphrodisiac effect, one of the sunamites was a blond, the other a brunette.

Rétif names as among the clients of Madame Janus an old banker, a rich merchant, a duke, a marshal of France, and a "médecine millionaire." And if Madame Janus had been previously known she would undoubtedly have lengthened the lives of Voltaire, Rousseau, Diderot, d'Alembert, Montesquieu and Fontenelle.

The nineteenth century, the century of natural science, also believed in the lengthening effects on life of sunamitism. One of the most famous cases is that of a rich prince who at a very advanced age always slept between two wet-nurses and fed himself from their breasts. This refinement seems to have been more common in the nineteenth century than the biblical custom. This may perhaps have been due to the decrial of the simple old fashioned lore of the ancients by modern science.

At any rate a modern scientist, Baco, has seriously declared that the reason teachers live so long is due to the fact that they are continually in the company of youth. According to Jaeger this opinion is widespread among the populace and indeed the latter believes that teachers of girls' schools live longer than those of boys' because the continual inhaling of girls' perspiration is healthier than that of boys.

"The therapeutic and macrobiotic value of sunamitism," says Hagen, "is naturally completely problematic. Modern science has discovered no fact that would tend to show that the perspiration of young persons on old ones tends to lengthen and renew life. When it is considered that the sunamites must have the good qualities of youth, health and beauty it seems but natural for this union to have a favorable effect on weak, old persons just as everything that is fresh and healthy has an exciting effect on man. At its best sunamitism is a kind of suggestional therapy and it is very improbable that the perspiration of young persons has a positive effect."

We are unable to wholly agree with this judgment of Hagen's. We see the essence in sunamitism, next to the suggestive element, in the natural body warmth. Just as helpful as hot bags and hot footbaths can be in the weakened condition of old age, so can the natural warmth of young bodies be useful for increasing the circulation of the blood and invigorating the weakened heart.

§ 3

OSPHRESIOLOGICAL LOVE CHARMS

Most love charms are naturally pure superstition. But it cannot be denied that there are some which really have a natural effect: usually those that depend on the sense of smell. Those notable forms of love charms in which sweat and other physical secretions are mixed for purposes of enchantment are to be explained by their effect on the sense of smell.

To healthy persons most odors of the body are no less than enchanting. But there are innumerable peculiarities in preferences for certain smells which often powerfully move the normal man; to persons of diseased minds the sweat of the body often becomes an irresistible excitant of love. Let us hear Krafft-Ebing on this point:

"It cannot be denied that the sense of smell is somehow connected with sexual perversions. The odor of flowers often excites passionate sensations; we need but recall the wise observation of Solomon in his *Song of Songs*: 'I rose up to open to my beloved: and my hands dropped with myrrh and my fingers with sweet smelling myrrh upon the handles of the lock.' In the Orient perfumes are greatly favored on account of their relation to the sexual parts. The wives of the sultan literally wallow in a sea of flowers."

Professor Most, of Rostock relates: "I discovered from a passionate young peasant that he had excited many modest maidens and easily succeeded in attaining his desires by placing his handkerchief under his armpit for a time during a dance, and then wiping the sweat off the face of his partner after a fast moving waltz."

That the odor of perspiration may give rise to a passionate affair is shown by the case of Henry III., who accidently dried his face with the slip of Marie de Clèves during the betrothal of the King of Navarre with Margaret de Valois. Although Marie was the bride of the Prince de Condé, Henry became so enamoured of her that he was unable to rest until both were plunged into the deepest misfortune, as is historically well-known. A similar tale is told of Henry IV., whose passion for the beautiful Gabrielle is said to have arisen when he dried his forehead with her handkerchief during a ball.

In this respect a custom reported by Jaeger on the Philippine Islands is worthy of note. If a couple must separate for some time due to a fishing expedition or the like, they give each other a slight garment of daily use. They promise eternal fidelity, carefully fold the objects, kiss them and — smell them very closely.

The preference of libertines and passionate women for perfumes should be sufficient witness for the relation between the sense of smell and the sexual sense.

§ 4

MEDIEVAL LOVE COURTS
PRINCESSES AS INSTRUCTRESSES IN SCIENCE OF LOVE
SIXTY FEMALE COUNSELLORS
BOLD LAWS AND DICTA OF THE CODEX OF LOVE

The Love-Courts of the Middle Ages were a reaction against the stringencies of Christianity. Their knighthood combined, if one may lay trust to the theories of J. de la Porte du Theil, love with ideal and practical piousness. A troubador of the thirteenth century would say that he would have candles lit and masses read so that his love might prove successful. This adaptation of religion to different erotic desires spread extraordinarily until they were even found in use in the court of Henry II. In his reign, men first started carrying in their prayer books pictures of their mistresses under the likeness of the holy Virgin, while the women would carry the picture of their lover under the likeness of Christ or some one of the saints.

Fauriel openly declares that the love-courts did not merely indulge in customary poetical problems but were much more interested in the most intimate and passionate occurrences of life. They ruled the most delicate relationship between the two sexes and thus had great influence upon the most respectable classes of society. André Le Chapelain describes in his work *De arte amatoria* the love-palaces in which the lovers would live eternally in the next world; either a paradise, a purgatory or a hell, according to their erotic conception here on earth.

The love-courts strove to rehabilitate sex and love against the moral precepts of Christianity. At the time of Charles VI., it was a kind of gallant reunion or society whose purpose was to represent the court of the God or the Goddesses of Love. A poem by Froissart entitled *Paradise of Love* refers to an actual Love-Court. A young knight had been repulsed by his mistress on some fancied score; enraged he asked the judges of the love-court for love-damages. His case was heard and his complaint was held justified. As punishment she was forced to do his bidding one night every week.

The existence of the love-courts has been a moot point for many years. Dietz has declared that it is a pure figment of the phantasy. But his chief proof falls to the ground since the *Erotica* of Andreas Capellanus, from which the love-courts are proven, are older than the savant assumes and actually belong to the thirteenth century. Thus today Weinhold grants the existence of the love-courts and the well-known French historian writes: "This sole remaining arrangement, the love-courts, was taken seriously by the respectable court ladies of the twelfth and thirteenth centuries in various parts of Provence, Aquitania and France. Love, which pretended to be a science and a religion, had its lawbook, its canon rights, and the feminine tribunals essayed to apply these rights.

The most grandiloquent of all these instructresses of

the science of love was Alienor or Cleonora of Aquitania. She was born sometime in the first two decades of the twelfth century and was married to the young king of France, Louis VII., in 1137. This princess stood, as Meray said, in the very heat of the fiery battles of love. She had illustrated six decrees in the book of Andreas Capellanus and belonged to those who contributed most to transforming the program of reformation of love and sex into actual life. The queen Alienor was moved by love and its problems until a very advanced age. She was sung of in ecstatic praise in Normandy by Bernard de Ventadour.

The boldest and most active person in the promulgation of the codex of love was Marie de Champagne, the daughter of Queen Alienor. Most of the judgments in cases of precedence that have come down to us are due to her. As the protectress and patroness of Andreas Capellanus, his entire book is inspired by her vivacious personality. Her court was great; she herself stated that it consisted of more than sixty female counsellors.

The love-courts of these high ladies, though perhaps the most respectable, were certainly not the only ones. Many women in society who did not occupy such high positions as the preceding, undoubtedly presided over love-courts of lesser importance. Not until much later do the love-courts of Provence and Avignon arise; the main historian is Jean Nostradamus. But it can easily be conceived that the bold laws of the codex of love could not find great influence in the close proximity of the papal residence at Avenor. Gradually the entire affair degenerated into a merry ceremony and into a great play, finally becoming a scene of nothing more than kisses and embraces. Even the presidency was no longer held by the women and princesses; masters and knights sat as counsellors next to the women. The love-courts were also only summoned to argue with those that came before it; to decide the problems that had come up and no longer to deliver actual decrees. They became mere poetic societies in which respectable ladies participated.

Andreas Capellanus has left us a collection of twenty-one of these dicta and the Codex of Love itself. This is a literary monument of the highest cultural value and we owe great thanks to the Frenchman, Meray, for having recognized its historic significance and having rescued it from the dust of the curio cabinet into which it had disappeared. What regard the Codex of Love enjoyed or at least what regard the ladies of the knighthood attempted to give it are proven by the legends bound up with its origin. Like all holy books this one must have a mysterious origin, and it is conceivable that this bible of knightly gallantry was connected with the court of Arthur, just as all ideals of the age of knighthood found their splendid prototype in his society.

We cite the following dicta from the Codex of Love:

1.

"Marriage is no hindrance to love."

This was the most mighty attack against the founda-

Bold Laws and Dicta

tions of social life and seems to have been directed by the women themselves against the husband with his ideals of faithfulness. This proposition was most often invoked by the women against the indifference of the husband or the refusal of the lover to break the bonds of marriage.

2.
"He who is not reticent is not worth loving."

6.
"Man shall not practice love until he is fully grown."

26.
"Love refuses love nothing."

As ideal as this dictum may appear on first glance, one should not be deceived into thinking that love in the days of knighthood was purely platonic. Were the lover to seek to fulfill all the wishes of the moods of his lady, or at least to make the attempt to do so, it must be remembered that even the most ideal knight is but a man!

We also cite some of the typical cases appearing before the Love-Courts as recorded by Andreas Capellanus:

Whether he has offended who has received permission from his lady to pay court to another and has failed to do so?

A knight received his desires from a lady by promising eternal love to her. He asked permission from his wife to pay court to another woman and to be allowed to receive her love. The wife gave him the permission. He departed and remained away a longer time than he had ever done before. Not until a month had passed did he return to his wife and confess that he had not wooed another woman but that he had merely wanted to put her to the test. His enraged wife then renounced her love and said this was sufficient grounds for divorce.

The love-queen handed down the following judgment:

We know that very often someone in love apparently desires that which his heart actually does not want at all, simply because he wishes to test the virtue of his wife; but he who thus deprives her body of every pleasure and joy while taking all these to himself, becomes a sinner on the part of true love. Granted.

Another judgment:

"When a woman marries her lover then her love is broken."

A lady had two knights as lovers. She gave herself up entirely to the second. Sometime afterwards in true feminine fashion, she married the first. Thereupon the sceond knight asked if she wished to continue his services. The wife declared she no longer had need of him since her love was all for her husband. Upon complaint to the love-queen the following decision resulted:

No true love is possible between married couples and

hence the lady defendant must give herself to the second knight and hold true to the love which she promised him.

SUPPLEMENT

A decision of the princess de Campania on whether true love can exist between married couples.

The princess decided that no true love could exist between married people because an unmarried couple did all the things they wanted in love from voluntary reasons and not because of law and order. A married couple, however, are promised to one another and are forced to do one another's will. What sort of honor is it to the husband or wife if he or she rejoices during the embrace and intercourse if it does not occur without legal permission, if when the fruits of love fall to them they must promise it to the state. The God of Love crowns his true devotees and initiates only when they are not yoked to the marriage chariot.

CHAPTER SIXTEEN

MYSTIC PHILOSOPHY OF COPULATION

§ 1

Sex, the Law of the Universe

CREATIVE nature has placed the highest pleasure in the union of the two sexes; and it is on this attraction, stretching from humanity to the animal kingdom, that there rests the certainty of the eternal victory of life over death. This attraction, sex, love, under whatever name it may masquerade, is the universal energy.

Jollivet-Castelot enthusiastically cries out: "It is sex that sustains and leads the astral worlds, the immense suns, the constellations, in steadfast gravitation; it is sex that encircles the universe in ether; it is sex that holds the balance, that rules the harmony in nature; it is sex that produces the passions, the lusts, the joys, and the sensual pleasures. Sex joins the lips of lovers, determines the courses of the waves, impregnates the flower and animal kingdoms, bring forth the smile and then the inexpressible frenzy of passion of the young woman in the embraces of her knowing lover."

It is love and sex alone that rule the world. What other sustenance need lovers in the first flushes of all-

Sex, the Law of the Universe

consuming madness? Eugène Nus has aptly captured this spirit in the following famous lines:

> "La loi d'amour est souveraine;
> Partout son doux verbe est écrit;
> Elle féconde, unit, entraîne
> La matière comme l'esprit.
> La terre s'échauffe à vos flammes
> Les cieux modulent vos accords.
> Amour, attraction des âmes,
> Attraction, amour des corps!"

The ancients, in fact, saw manifestations of the all-embracing sex in every phenomenon of nature. We read in the *Prem Sagar, A Boat in the Ocean of Love*: "Then did the clouds refreshen the earth with showers of rain like unto a husband with his spending of semen. Both, eight long months separated from the husband, eagerly drank in the birth-giving potion and proudly displayed their refreshened and bedewed groins unto him."

Like an echo of the Indian poet, Virgil cries out in his symbolic language: "The modest heaven burns with love for the earth, who prepares herself for his passionate embrace..."

§ 2

IMMEMORIAL CONECPTIONS OF SEX
VEDIC LOVE IN INDIA
FESTIVALS OF THE LINGAM AND PHALLUS

This great law of sex masters and rules the world. No religion has at any time been able to escape it. Sex indeed played an extremely important rôle in the ancient religions. With the exception of the Iranians and the Jews, the entire period of antiquity held sexual intercourse to be perfectly permissible, as long as no rights were injured.

The Vedic conception of sex is completely naturalistic in spite of the shrouds of poesy with which the Indian enwraps himself. "Vedic Love," says Marius Fontane, "was of exceptional purity because it was completely free and absolutely frank. The lovers made known their mutual attraction and the man fulfilled the desires of the girl. Thus the male did not abuse his potency and the female did not sacrifice her charm. No unhealthy coquetry, no feelings of domination. The Vedic law seems to have well understood the nature and course of sex."

In the *Rig-Veda*, Syavaswa invokes the night to bring gifts to the beautiful Darbha and her father: "The moon is the constellation of love; under its white rays there arises that soft dreamery that excludes sensual ardor and debasing passion. The highest joy to the Arian is the softly impressed kiss on the trembling cheek while the girl assumes the position of the friend who whispers softly into the ear of the lover."

In India the God of Love and the symbol of sex is Kamadeva, who sprang forth fully armed from the flaming heart of Brahma, just as Minerva from the forehead of Jupiter. The bow of Kamadeva is made of flowers, his strings are formed from bees, at the head

Vedic Love in India

of his five arrows there is a flower which presents a meaning to all. Kamadeva is the ruler of the *apsaras* or the holy nymphs. He has many names: god of lust, exciter of the spirit, of madness, the inflamer, the disturber of pious rest, and the bodiless.

Granted eternal youth and incomparable beauty, he practices his domination over gods and men alike. Krishna, whose erotic deeds are sung of in the *Prem Sagar*, is also the God of Love of the Hindus. But Siva is the god to whom most of the shrines are dedicated, the favorite symbol of the Siva cult being the lingam.

This replica of the male progenitive organ is found in great abundance at Cambodia, where every year at the celebration of the arrival of spring an immense hollow lingam is led about in a procession on the streets. A young boy is hidden within it and at times makes the appropriate movements as if engaged in the sexual act.

The yogis wear the lingam around their necks and always offer it the first fruits of all their feasts. The masculine member is looked upon by all the people of ancient times as the symbol of universal fructification. Its cult has grown to one of the most popular myths of India. The legends tell us that the God Siva lives upon the Mountain of Gold, Kailasa; there upon a terrace is a very handsome table decorated with the most costly of stones; in the center of the table is a lotus flower, and in the center of the lotus flower there is a triangle, the origin and the source of all things.

From this triangle there proceeds a lingam, the eternal

god, who makes his eternal home in this residence.

Even today, after three thousand years, in spite of the puritanism of England, the Hindus still worship these geometrical symbols of the lingam and the yoni. One sees the lingam everywhere; in streets, roads, byways, public squares, fields, etc. The religious ceremonies are always impregnated with these same erotic tendencies.

Let us turn for a moment to Benares, the holy city of the Hindus. The sun arises. It is the hour for ablutions. And no water is holier and healthier than that of the Ganges. The men, women and children walk down the great stairways to the river and dip themselves in its holy waters which wash away all their pollutions and defilements. The women throw garlands of flowers into the river so that it almost seems to be a flowing green-house. Fakirs, as immovable as marble columns, stand lost in mute contemplation, with one hand stretched out to the rising sun. From the heights of the terrace the Brahmins exhibit the holy lingams to the mass. On the other side of the river the decaying architecture of the palaces draws itself to the blue skies. The temples arise with their pyramids of cut-stone whereon are portrayed the images of the gods and of the symbolic and sacred animals. Everywhere is an extravagance of sculpture, a monstrous floresence of stone. Within the halls there cower enormous cattle made of marble. Then the almost infinitely repeated image of Graneças, the god of wisdom, the god with the elephant's head.

Festivals of the Lingam and Phallus 247

The ablutions are completed; the music resounds from the temple; the populace mass their way in. The marble columns with their graven images of the gods are decorated with flowers, but practically all of the gifts are brought to the lingam, which the women crown with velvet flowers moistened with dissolved butter. They rise about the temple, in every stretch and corner. Fakirs promenade about entirely naked, their bodies besmeared with cow-dung. Others haunch themselves down in the position of corpses as naked as the former and covered only by the traditional cow-dung.

All around the temple are carried on palanquins images of Siva; Siva the word, and Siva the power. The god, is whose indeterminate form (male and female alike) carries in one hand a lingam, in the other a phallus of gold. The priests clad in white, awe-inspiring, bear aloft the phallic emblems, before which the people prostrate themselves.

In front, in the midst of the flute players, prance about the bayaderes, their arms bare, their knuckles surrounded with silver bracelets, their fingers and toes loaded down with rings and an immense gold ring hanging down from the right side of the nose. They rhythmically sway their hips about, and silver bells attached to the flanges of their dress, musically tinkle throughout the hall. In the temple a Brahman with naked head crosses his legs and cries out: "I am Brahma, I am the All."

To the soft rhythm of the flutes and tomtoms the

bayaderes turn themselves about and wildly gyrate themselves into sacred dislocations. Meanwhile the Brahmins have had brought the sacred phalli, heavily silvered and decorated with jewelry. The believers worshipfully kiss them and moisten them with water from the Ganges. The women in hysteric positions embrace the monstrous symbol, frenziedly kiss it, and crown it with flowers. The sacred cows with the golden horns move through the mass. Thereupon the Brahman arises and cries: "We have washed ourselves pure in the filth of sins: Make us fruitful and fortunate." And, touching his navel and genital organ, he adds: "There dwells the fire, the sun and the moon."

Now he relates to the worshipful listeners, who have meanwhile smeared themselves with cow-dung, the wondrous story of Krishna, who at the age of fifteen years had seduced and laid low all the cowherdesses of the country; he praises the powers of Siva, who unceasingly creates and destroys as the symbol of nature.

In his description of the erotic ceremonies of India, Windsor notes the "custom of the left hand," which unites the two sexes and temporarily allows all distinctions between castes to be forgotten. In this secret orgy the participants, gorged with meat and spirituous drinks, worship the Sakti[1] in the form of a woman; she is completely disrobed and placed upon a kind of pedestal; an initiate completing the sacrifice by the sexual act.

---

[1] Sakti-potency; sensual manifestation of Siva, is viewed as the feminine half of this divinity.

The ceremonies usually end with general cohabitation, each pair representing and becoming identical with Siva and his Sakti. The believers must fulfill these actions, their thoughts having arisen to divine planes and theoretically disconnected from the mere satisfaction of sensuality. The precepts teaching these customs are full of devout moral theories, and are supposed to be fulfilled even by ascetics.

Chinese Buddhism contains a great part of the erotic symbolism of Indian Buddhism. It proceeds from the system of Mahayana, believes in a paradise, a sea of lotus flowers, where the sages are reborn, and calls it *ngyan lo* (pleasure), *kyo lo* (kingdom of pleasure), *tsing tu* (glorious land).

§ 3

ZOROASTER

AND

PRAYER IN THE PURITY OF LOVE

Zoroaster commands purification of the sexual act by prayer. Although he punishes infanticide and concubinage with death, he bears no ill-will against "such lustful women who make public engagements, stop on their way and nourish themselves on whatever fate sends them."

The moral endeavors of the Mazdeer, his conception of love, of duty, and of human fate are to be found in the following prayer: "I entreat thee, O Ormuzd, for joy, purity, and holiness. Grant me a long and well applied life. Give unto man pure and healthy joys so that he will always remain procreative and thus in the best of good spirits."

§ 4

SEX IN THE CHALDEAN RELIGIONS

Physical love also assumed an important part of the religious views of the ancient Chaldeans. Nebuchadnezzar turned to the god Merodoch and begged for "a sevenfold fecundity." When the Chaldeans turned to their wives, they became far more realistic; the literal translation of an inscription found in the alcove of a woman's room reads: "Ouvre ta vulve, pour que je puisse assouvir mes désirs." In relation to pregnant and nursing women they had the following formula: "If you approach a pregnant woman, her womb protruding, all disordered, and firmly convinced that she will not give birth, then invoke against all this the mystic names of the earth and of the heavens and everything shall disappear."

§ 5

SEX IN THE ASSYRIAN RELIGIONS
PRIESTS OF BAAL

In the Assyrian religion Belit, Sin, and Istar represent divinities who often have sexual intercourse with one another: the fructifying power, the idealization of passion, the goddess of love. Rare fragments of Assyrian literature tell us of the love of Thammuz and Istar, whose *dénouement,* the tragic death of Thammuz, had a remarkable parallel in the poetic legend of the death of Adonis, who like him was killed in a mountain by a wild animal and was bewailed by the goddess of love and the inconsolable nymphs.

The Assyrians also worshipped Baal Peor or Belphegor, a god something like Priapus, whose temples degenerated into places of debauchery. Rosenbaum states in his *Geschichte der Lustseuche im Altertum* that the name Baal Peor means in Hebrew "the God Penis," the Priapus of the Romans." His temple stood on the mountain Peor and the young maidens would come there in order to prostitute themselves. This cult was similar to that of the lingam in India and of the phallus in Asia.

The Phœnician priests and prophets of Baal and of Astarte dressed themselves as women, rouged their faces and eyes. In the frenzy of their religious dilirium they went so far as mutilating their own bodies. The priestesses gave themselves up to public prostitution in honor of Astarte. According to Dufour's *Histoire de la Prostitution* the pederastic priests of Baal were handsome, unbearded young men, their entire bodies being depilated and perfumed with fragrant salves. They carried on a secret trade of their virginity in the shrine of Baal. The Vulgata calls them "effeminati," in Hebraic they are called "Kedeschim," signifying initiate or saint. Their usual duties consisted of the more or less active application of their infamous mysteries. They sold themselves to the worshippers of their god and placed upon his altars the wages of their prostitution.

The young men even went so far as to sell the services of a dog trained for the same shameful ends and inquired from every worshipper whether he had any desires for the dog-service.

§ 6

SEX AND THE RELIGIONS OF EGYPT
ISIS FESTIVALS

Egypt, the ancient mother of the divine arts and fables, was a center for the mysteries of Isis. Herodotus states that every year seven hundred thousand pilgrims came to Bubastis during the festivals of Isis.

Dupouy, in his *Ancient Prostitution*, writes that the priests of the goddess carried a mystic winnow containing corn and bran. The priests of the god carried the sacred *Tau* or the key opening the best guarded castle. This *Tau* represented the masculine member, the winnow (also an ear of corn) the feminine sexual organ. In addition there passed by an *eye*, with or without brows, representing the attributes of Osiris, in order to point out clearly the connection between the two sexes. Initiated young maidens, called *cistophores* (fruit basket carriers) carried mystic *ciste* (rush baskets). Immediately after them came a priestess who carried in her bosom a golden urn containing a phallus. Dulaure states in his interesting work *Des divinités génératrices* that these rush baskets contained a great variety of obscene cakes and breads in the form of male and female genitals.

§ 7

Cult of the Phallus
Dionysian Festivals
Cult of Cotytto and Nymphomania

The cult of phallus and Priapus stood in great honor throughout Greece and later in Rome and all Italy. According to Berard, Hermes is represented in Greece by a bust on a half column almost always equipped with an immense erect phallus; this *cippus* of classical times is only the perfected form of the coarse stone placed into the earth like a Breton relic of a Druid (Menhir). These semi-columns are nothing but the *Ancab* of the Arabians, the *Neçib* of the Phœnicians, the *Hammanin* of the Hebrews, sacred stones which the semite worshipped as the image, or rather the dwelling, of the divinity Beth-el, from which arose the Greek Bætylia.

Vinson gives the simple proof that the phallic cult, viewed as a symbol of procreation, represents one of the most notable religious forms. He adds that no obscenity is present in this worship; it is a simple honor to natural instinct and natural need, the monition to an important and necessary phenomenon. Everywhere can be discovered the cult of phallus or traces of it: in West Africa, among the Papuas of New Guinea, who decorated the tops of their roofs with immense images of male and female genitals to the great embarrassment of the European visitors; upon the islands of the South Seas, where great black stones and even trees are honored as symbols of generation.

In Arabia we came across the grave of a famous sheik whose monument consisted of an enormously great phallus made of basalt and which had been perceptibly worn away by the kisses of women who hoped in this manner to attain the fecundity denied them by nature. Even in England, in the neighborhood of Durham, there are public traces of this cult in the customs of the people. The notorious Jack, of Hilton near Birmingham, appears to be but a phallic idol.

Dionysian Festivals

Plutarch mentions that even at the first festivals of Dionysus a phallus was present in honor of Bacchus. The erotic character of this festival became increasingly strengthened with time.

The epopts, initiates in the mysteries, marched in front of the parade. Male and female Bacchantes rode on asses and goats, their hair flying in the wind, their countenances distorted, swaying immense phalli in an erect state. Then came the *canephore*, virgin priestesses, who carried golden baskets filled with the first crops, all surrounded with miniature phalli. Then followed the *phallophore*, the head entirely covered with ivy, violets, thymes, and acanthus; they also carried enormous images of the genitals and surrounded a statue of Bacchus distinguished by a triple phallus made of figwood (*triphallus*).

The festival of Adonis was but a pretense for prostitution. In tents decorated with myrtle and laurel leaves the *hierodule* priestesses of the goddess, young and beautiful Greek and Syrian slaves, would pause for the spectators. They were covered with gems and trinkets, clothed with rich material, a rich mitre decorated their heads, their long black tresses were interwoven with flowers and a scarlet band fluttered over their shoulders. On their beautifully rounded bosoms hung trinkets of gold and pearls; as a token of their religious service they held a branch of myrtle and a dove, sacred to Venus, in their hand. During this festival all women were constrained to cut off their hair or to give themselves up for one day to strangers in honor of the goddess (Astarte or Anaïtis), in face of the statue of the god, which for this occasion was surrounded with an unlimited number of phalli of different sizes. They gave themselves up to the embraces of strangers, says Lucian, as often as one would pay them, and all the money brought in by this public prostitution was applied to a sacrifice for Anaïtis. The cult of *cotytto* rapidly spread from Thrace and Phrygia to Greece.

Pindar and Plutarch both agree that women were often given to a goat for purposes of sexual intercourse in honor of Mendes, the goat.

Villemont also assures us that women who suffered from nymphomania were shut in the temples with these animals and were let out only when the goats were incapable of any longer fulfilling their desires.

§ 8

The Corybantes
Cult of Priapus in Rome

It was the Corybantes or priests of Cybele, who transplanted the phallic cult from Phrygia to Etruria. In a learned treatise Dupouy has shown that it was the Etruscans who passed on to the Romans these new religious institutions with their ceremonies and practices. The

Cult of Priapus in Rome 257

time of the introduction of this cult in Rome does not appear to be very ancient for its inhabitants were not acquainted with the cult of Venus at the time of its emperor. Those of Bacchus and of Priapus also appear to have been unknown to them. The best proof that for a certain time the cult of Priapus was localized in Etruria lies in an expression of Atheneus, that the Etrucians led a very immoral life; that the Messapians, the Samnites and the Lokrians and other peoples of Latium prostituted their daughters freely, but that the Romans did not.

Dupouy adds: "There still exists in Etruria a cult similar to that of the Indian lingam and the Asiatic phallus. Both have the same purpose: the defloration of virgins before marriage as a part of sacred prostitution. This Etruscan god, of whom we know not from historical monuments, but from the writings of Arnobius and Saint Augustine, was named Mutunus and Mutuna, for he had both a masculine and a feminine side."

In Rome the phallic symbol was the god Priapus, who was represented with an erect penis of fantastic dimensions. This phallus was almost always made of wood, either cyprus or fig-tree. The men brought the first fruits of their gardens to Priapus and turned to him for cures. Then the measurements of their members in the form of a phallus were hung about his statue. The women who took recourse to Isis filled the temples with similar *ex-votos*, which, however, represented the feminine genitals. A patient accompanied the present of one of these priapic *ex-votos* with the following:

VOTI SOLUTIO

"Cur pictum memori sit in tabella
Membrum quæritis, unde procreamur?
Cum penis mihi forte læsus esset,
Chirurgique manum miser timerem,
Dis me legitimis nimisque magnis,
Ut Phæbo, puta filioque Phæbi,
Curatum dare mentulam verebar."

"You ask why people bring as votive offerings images of the sexual offerings that created us? Hear me! My penis has been seriously damaged and I, unfortunate creature, fear the knife of the surgeon. Still less durst I turn to those of our gods whose art is of healing, to Apollo, and his son Aesculapius; for they are too illustrious and it would appear to me to be too presumptuous to turn to them for the curing of my poor, ailing member."

The unfortunate hence applied to the mercies of Priapus, the god-protector of his sexual member. "If thou curest me without the frightful amputation of my penis, I will have painted a picture of the organ that thou hast saved for me and will honor it in thy name. The image will correspond exactly to my original in length, circumference, shape and color. If this is agreeable to thee, give me some token and thou shalt have my vow."

It was a custom in Rome for the young virgins to be

Cult of Priapus in Rome

led into the garden of Priapus before they embraced the nuptial couch of their husbands, so that they could sacrifice their virginity to the god. The virgin was placed on the *fascinum,* i.e., the immense, upright penis of the god's statue, so that she might become fruitful by this divine principle. This symbolic action was also very often completed by the physical act.

In an ancient poem to Priapus (*Priapi Carmen*) a noble Roman lady sacrifices images of elephants to the god and solemnly begs him to grant her the joys that he controls and which were there described in almost every possible situation.

It should finally be mentioned that the phalli were also worn as amulets and were even hung about the necks of children. The majority of these had a pair of wings and were decorated with tiny tinkling bells. The museum at Naples has a special private room in which are to be seen an immense number of objects of all kinds, each one being in the shape of a penis.

§ 9

Cult in Venus

Spiritual Union and the Goddess of Sex

Has the reader ever seen in the Uffcia at Florence that masterpiece of Cleomenes, son of Apollodorus of Athens, the Medicean Venus, this image of passion and supreme bliss, this pagan Eve whose left hand would try to serve the same purpose as the fig-leaf. Or in the

National Museum at Naples, next to the harsh and ancient bust of the Farnese Juno, that divine marble in which life, grace and love shimmer in ecstatic unison: Venus Callipygos, that most beautiful, vivacious, passionate and desirable of all the Venuses of ancient times?

Venus or Aphrodite, Paphia or Cytherea, Anadyomene or Genetrix, it is always the one whom Paris crowned as queen whose beauty arose from the depths of the azure sea, who was worshipped by the Greeks and Romans enlightened by art and literature, for she idolized the flesh and explained the body of woman by her erotic poesy. Whom else should Lucretius invoke in his *De rerum natura*,

> "*Mother of Rome, delight of gods and men,*
> *Dear Venus that beneath the gliding stars*
> *Makest to teem the many voyaged main*
> *And fruitful lands — for all of living things*
> *Through thee alone are evermore conceived,*
> *Before thee, Goddess, and thy coming on,*
> *Flee stormy wind and massy cloud away,*
> *For thee the deadal earth bears scented flowers,*
> *For thee the waters of the unvexed deep*
> *Smile, and the hollows of the serene sky*
> *Glow with diffused radiance for thee!*
> *For soon as comes the springtime face of day,*
> *And procreant gales blow from the West unbarred,*
> *First fowls of air, smit to the heart by thee,*
> *Foretoken thy approach, I thou Divine,*

*And leap the wild herds round the happy fields
Or swim the bounding torrents. Thus amain,
Seized with the spell, all creatures follow thee
Whithersoever thou walkest forth to lead,
And thence through seas and mountains and swift
    streams,
Through leafy homes of birds and greening plains,
Kindling the lure of love in every breast,
Thou bringest the eternal generations forth,
Kind after kind."*

Venus was the most radiant creation of Greece. Even today there is more than one pagan who yearns for her return. Lajard in his authoritative work in the cults of Venus assures us that her reign has not yet been completely extinguished. He reports that the Druses of Libanon have dedicated an actual cult to the worship of the feminine genital organ and that services are held in her honor every Friday morning, that day dedicated to Venus and on which the Mussulman has enjoined on him by the law-book of Mohammed the double duty of attending the mosques and fulfilling his marital duty to his wife the same evening.

The Nozaire, who have retained the ceremony of worship and service to Cteis, believe that the sexual act is the only means by which spiritual union can be completely attained.

The cult seems also to have been retained by certain peoples of Oceania. The Areois of Tahiti seem to have formed a pattern for other tribes, according to Westermarck. Their life is dedicated to debauchery and in honor to the goddess of sex, whose divine services consist of the most obscene dances and pantomimes with men and beasts alike. The Oulitaos have gone so far as to form special societies, whose sole purpose is epicureanism. They have a special secret and allegoric language, the words of which are mostly sexual and of an obscene nature. At their divine festivals they gather round an immense statue of a woman cunningly contrived so as to form an image of a penis.

§ 10

SEX IN THE RELIGIONS OF NORDIC COUNTRIES

In the religions of almost all these peoples traces of sex and love cults can be found. In Armenia, Lydia, Persia, and Scythia the people worship Anaïtis, to whom are consecrated young virgins and who prostitute themselves in her honor.

In Sweden and Germania, Hertha was the goddess of fecundity. The cold Scandinavians chose as goddess of love, beauty, grace and fecundity, the beautiful Freisa (Frida or Frigga), daughter of Njord, wife of the awesome Odin and daughter of Freyer, the Scandinavian Priapus, representative of the male principle. Friday is dedicated to this goddess, linking her to the Greek

Venus. She is also worshipped by the old inhabitants of Ireland.

Among the Lithuanians, the goddess of love and beauty bore the gracious name of Milda. Like Venus, she also had a gallant adventure with the god of war, the fearsome Kauas. Their son was called Kaunis, and the great city of Kovno was named after him. An exceedingly beautiful valley was dedicated to his mother and became the Lithuanian Cytherea.

The Rhagana, lower divinities, were also dedicated to love. These hamadryads reward with embraces those who save them from death by protecting them from the ax of the woodcutter, in felling trees, since their existence was connected to them.

Love and sex play an important rôle in the religious belief of the Lithuanians; they must beautify the future paradise especially promised to those warriors who fall in their country's service. "Beautiful women, good food and drink, perfect health and potency, constant merriness, laughter and play, these are the joys that await those fortunates on the other side of the grave. In order to completely enjoy these pleasures, their power is increased a hundredfold."

§ 11

Islam and Sex
Adoration of Sex
Sex-Act as Form of Prayer

According to Mohammed, the founder of the religion of Islam, god created man "by a drop of his sperm." Then he reveals to us the drama of the birth of the male (active) principle and the feminine (passive) principle:

"The male principle is first called Aïsh, the feminine Aïsha.

"But Adam, who divided himself into two parts, under the influence of the first tremblings of delight and of the perfumed and enervating joys of paradise, saw that Aïsha was beautiful; intoxicated by her beauty he took her unto himself and completed the first coition in his immense pride believing that he was accomplishing a divine action, and thereby produced the great human family.

"And at this great event it happened that Adam named the woman who was taken from his flesh, Eve, i.e., the mother of the human race.

"And Adam saw that coition was good, in that it gave the man as well as the woman inexpressible joy, and it also made of the man the active principle, the creator, a completer of the divine procreative will.

Islam and Sex

"And he also saw that coition was the basis of creation, its procreative and maintaining principle."

He further added:

"...When we contemplate the significance of this action, whose completion is the restoral of unity in that it fuses man and woman, we are moved to the conclusion that this act is the most significant of all those on earth that try to serve the splendor of the almighty God, who by an emanation of his will created the kingdoms of man, animal, plant and mineral..."

The savants and saints of Islam are a long way from those who consider coition as an act contrary to the laws of piety and religion. We read in the *Koran*: "Take unto thyself for wife a virgin who embraces thee and whom thou embracest. Do not begin coition without having first excited thyself by embraces." The prophet further says: "Thy women are thy cornfields. Plant thou thy corn zealously in them in service of thy creator."

"Coition, oh! man," we read in *El-Ktab*, "is the greatest and holiest song of praise — the highest desire of man and his companion for primitive unity and the paradisiacal joys. It is like the neighing of the stallion for the tent where he will find the food that he has earned after a long pursuit, fresh water whose murmuring is a sublime joy, and the restful quiet that will refreshen his members and lend him new strength for the morning's work."

This same savant of God often supports the sublime

and divine character of the sexual act. Thus after deciding that there are some profane persons who find only coarse, animal satisfaction in the act, he decries: "They have neither understood nor seen that sex-love is the *fiat lux* of the book of Moses; the divine law and the law for the preservation of all species, degrees, continents, seas, worlds and spaces; *the supernatural act par excellence,* a paradisiac memory; the most beautiful of all rhapsodies of praise directed to the creator by his creatures; the sufficient reason for life in all its expressions, the alpha and omega of all creation..."

Coition thus becomes a form of prayer and the man who satisfies his sexual instinct becomes a fellow-laborer of God, continuing the work of creation as a quasi-divine sower of seeds.

"O, true believers," cries the divine Kohdja Omer Aleby, "satisfy yourselves according to the precepts of the *Koran*, with your spirit, with your soul elevated to God; perform your sexual duty like a creator, like a mighty man in work and power who is conscious of the import of what he is doing, and you will have a twofold pleasure: an energetic flow of semen and the production of healthy and powerful children.

"Out of your satisfaction make it an act of creative power, a pleasant duty, in which you allow your wives to take part, so that you share with them your joys and your ennobled happiness."

In reality, he who loves sacrifices himself and the pleasure is his reward. Love is a complete martyrdom,

Islam and Sex

an absolute sacrifice of the individual for the species. Pleasure is only the means which the species has to attain its purpose, a veil to throw over the eyes of the individual to bring him to its sacrificial altar. The species forces the individual person by the illusion of pleasure to an action that will ensure posterity. "The physical lure of sex," says Hugues le Roux, "is a snare in which the individual is caught and plays the rôle of a marionette for the production of more and possibly better marionettes." Joanny Roux similarly notes that "the sexual manifestations of our individual interests are always opposed to one another."

Mohammed not only permitted and idealized love on earth but he also promised those who followed the way of Allah the most beautiful women in the next world. His paradise swarms with houris who with fiery embraces multiply the unabated sensual delight and afford eternal delight to the chosen people.

§ 12

SEX AS MISTRESS OF THE WORLD
SEX THE AMAZING MIRACLE OF ALL TIME

Paul de Régla aptly remarks in contemplating the different symbolic manifestations of sex in the magic wheel of time: "In all ages, the divinity who served as the symbol of procreation of the human race, that most amazing miracle of all times, received the most adoration and the most influential cults. Sex rules this world just as it led the old one. The Queen of Heaven may no longer live in Olympus, but in our hearts and souls we know that she has merely assumed a Christian form and feeds the flames of our fancies as she has done since the beginning of time. Love may be represented as a child like Cupid, or in the form of a phallus, or a sacred heart pierced by an arrow, or in a myriad different ways. But the mystic idea is always the same: Love, Sex, Eros, Venus."

FINIS

BIBLIOGRAPHY
of Works Used in
MAGICA SEXUALIS

BIBLIOGRAPHY
of Works Used in
MAGICA SEXUALIS

ALLEN-KARDEC.

ANDRÉ. *Lettres au sujet de la magie, des maléfices et des sorciers.*

AUBIN, N. *Histoire des diables de Loudun, ou de la possession des religieuses Ursulines et de la condamnation d'Urbain Grandier.*

AUGUSTINUS. *Oeuvres.*

BEKKER, BALTHASAR. *Die bezauberte Welt.*

BELLAIGUE. *Psychologie de la Musique.*

BERTHELOT. *La chimie au moyen âge.*

BERTHELOT. *Transmission de la science magique.*

BIZOUARD, J. *Des rapports de l'homme avec les démons.*

BLAN, L. *Das altjuedische Zauberwesen.*

BODIN, J. *De magorum daemonomania.*

BOEHME. *Geschichte des Tanzes.*

BONNIOT. *Le Miracle et ses contrefaçons.*

BRIERRE DE BOISMONT, A. *Des hallucinations ou hist. rais. des apparitions, des visions, des songes, de l'extase, des rêves, du magnétisme et du somnambulisme.*

BUREAU D'ADRESSES. *Recueil général des questions traitées et conférences du Bureau d'Adresses.*

CAMPANELLA, TH. *De sensu rerum et magia.*

CASAUBON, M. *A treatise proving spirits, witches and supernatural operations by pregnant instances and evidences.*
CHRISTIAN, P. *Histoire de la magie.*
CYPRIAN. *Démonologie.*
DARBLAY, PIERRE. *Physiologie de l'amour.*
DE LA MAUZE. *Remarques sur l'antiquité et l'origine de la Kabbale.*
DEBREYNE, R. P. *Moechialogie.*
DELRIO, MARTIN. *Disquisitiones magiae.*
DEL RIO, M. *Disquisitionum magicarum.*
DUFOUR. *History of Prostitution.*
DULAURE. *Gods of Generation.*
DUPOUY, E. *La prostitution dans l'antiquité.*
ESCHENMAYER, C. A. *Conflict zwischen Himmel und Hoelle, an dem Daemon eines bessessenen Maedchens beobachtet.*
FAUST, J. *Magia naturalia et innaturalia.*
FIGUIER. *Histoire du merveilleux.*
FREUD, S. *Die Traumdeutung.*
GAVET, D. *La magie maternelle.*
GOUGENOT DES MOUSSEAUX. *Les hauts phénomènes de la Magie.*
GRAETZ. *Geschichte der Juden.*
HORST, G. C. *Daemonomagia.*
HUYSMANS, J. K. *Là Bas.*
IBN-KHALDUN. *Prolegomena.*
IMMERMAN. *Der Karneval und die Somnambult.*
JACOBUS, REX ANGLIAE. *Daemonologia.*
JAMBLICHUS. *Die mysteriis Aegyptiorum, Chaldaeorum, Assyriorum*
JOLLIVET-CASTELOT. *La vie et l'âme de la matière.*

Kiesewetter, K. *Der occultismus des Altertums.*
Kiesewetter, K. *Die Geheimwissenschaften.*
Krafft-Ebing, R. von. *Experimentalische Studien.*
Lajard. *Recherches sur le culte de Vénus.*
Lancre, P. de. *Tableau de l'inconstance des mauvais anges et démons, traicté des sorcièrs, et de la sorcellerie.*
Légué. *Médecins et empoisonneurs.*
Leloyer, V. *Des Spectres.*
Lermina. *Magie pratique.*
Lévi, Eliphas. *La clef des grands mystéres suivant Henoch, Abraham, Hermès Trismégiste, et Salomon.*
Louandre. *Sorcellerie.*
Louvel, Réne. *Traité de chasteté.*
Magnus, Albertus. *Les admirables secrets cont. plusieurs traités sur la conception des femmes, des vertus des herbes, etc.*
Mannhart, W. *Zauberglaube und Geheimwissen.*
Marquardt, J. *Roman Cults.*
Menant, J. *Ninive et Babylone.*
Michelet. *La Sorcière.*
Mirandola, Pico della. *De promotione.*
Nogent, Guibert de. *De vita sua.*
Plytoff. *La Magie.*
Pontanus. *Urania sive de stellis.*
Prierias, Silvestre de. *Strigimagarum demonumque mirandis.*
Prost. *Les arts et les sciences occultes.*
Psellus, M. *De operatione daemonum.*
Régla, Paul de. *El-Ktab.*
Rosenbaum. *Geschichte der Lustseuche im Altertum.*
Roskoff, G. *Geschichte des Teufels.*

Roux, Joanny. *Psychologie de l'instinct sexuel.*
Smith, W. *The Demon.*
Sprenger, J. *Malleus maleficarum.*
Star, Ely. *Les mystères de l'horoscope.*
Tours, Grégoire de. *Oeuvres.*
Vaughan, Th. *Magia Adamica.*
Ventura. *La raison philosophique et la raison catholique.*
Vinson, J. *Les religions actuelles.*
Westermarck. *History of Human Marriage.*
Wier, J. *Histoires, disputes et discours des illusions et impostures des diables, des magiciens infâmes, sorcières et de la punition.*
Windsor, E. *Hindu Art of Love.*

A CABINET

OF

UNUSUAL ILLUSTRATIONS

ON

MAGICA SEXUALIS

THE TEMPTATION OF ST. ANTHONY

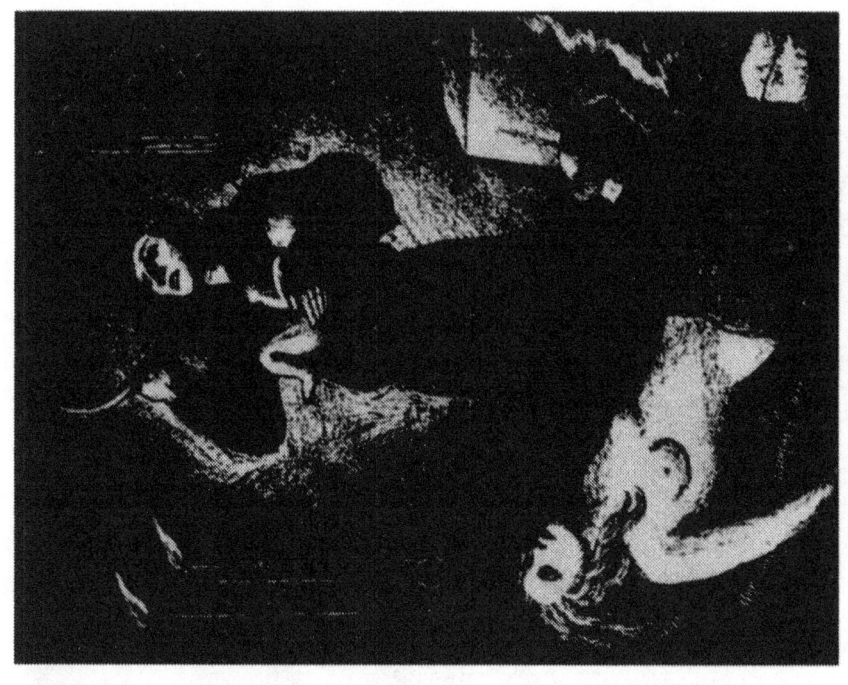

© Ives Washburn, Inc. (Theda Kenyon: *Witches Still Live*)
SECRET RITES OF THE BLACK MASS

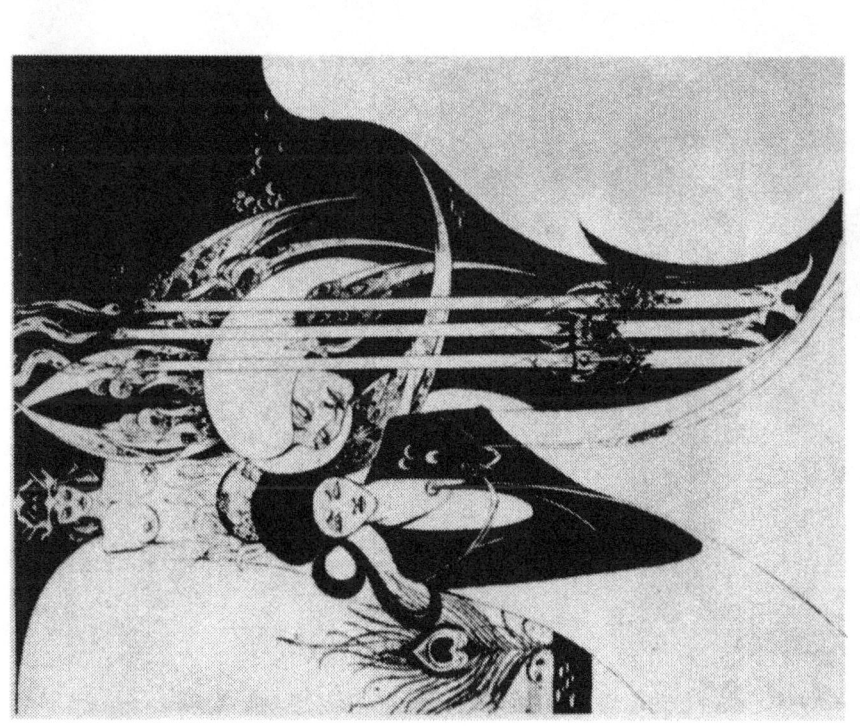

INITIATION INTO THE BLACK ART

THE GOAT MENDES PRESIDING OVER A DIABOLICAL EXPERIMENT

THE COURTS OF LOVE

EN ROUTE FOR THE "HEX" CONCLAVE

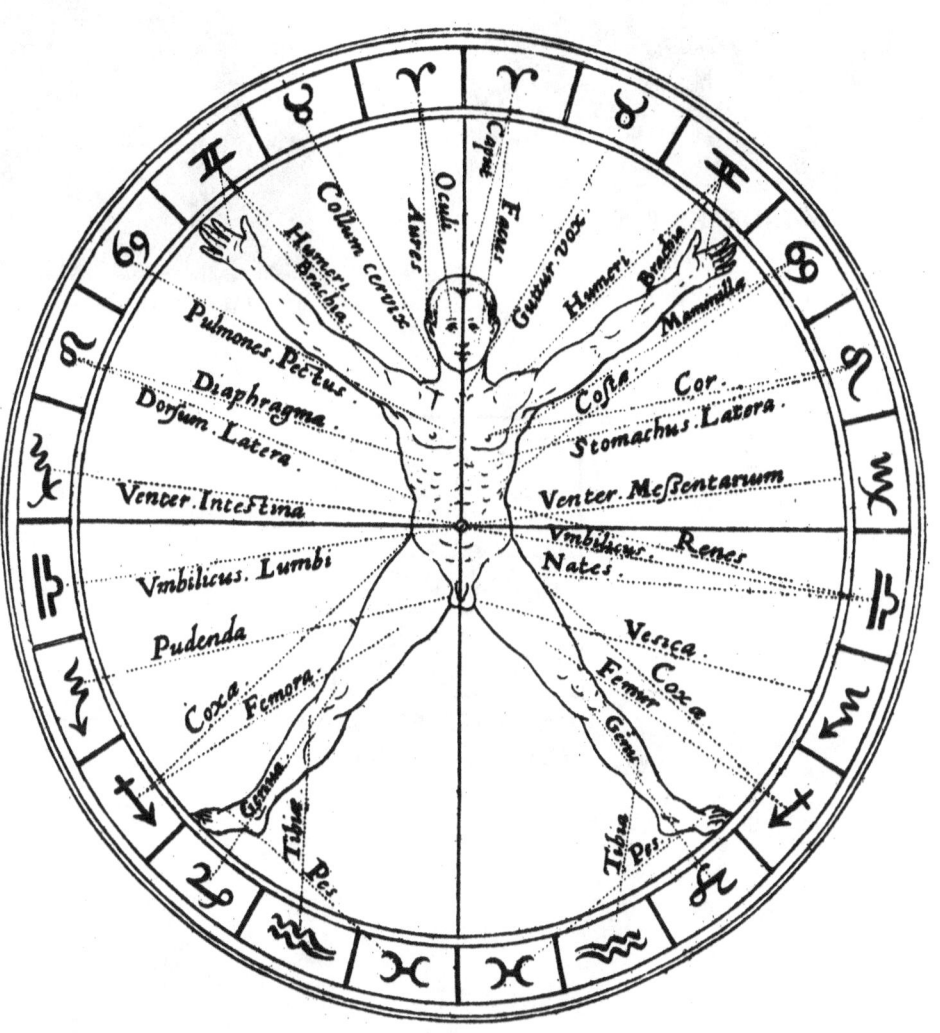

OCCULT ANATOMY

MANDRAKE ROOTS

TWO CARROTS

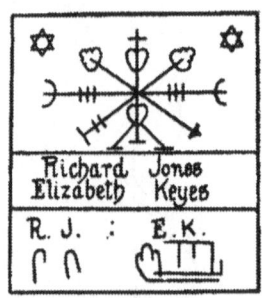

"A CHARACTER FOR LOVE"
(XVII Century MS.)

THE TRINITY; SALERNO,
XIII CENTURY

HINDU SEXUAL SYMBOLISM

THE DUCHESS OF GLOUCESTER CONSULTING A DEMON
(Henry VI; 1, 4)

(Scene from *Goona Goona*, First Division film)
APPROACHING THE SORCERER'S CAVE FOR THE "GOONA GOONA"
OR LOVE-POWDER; ISLAND OF BALI

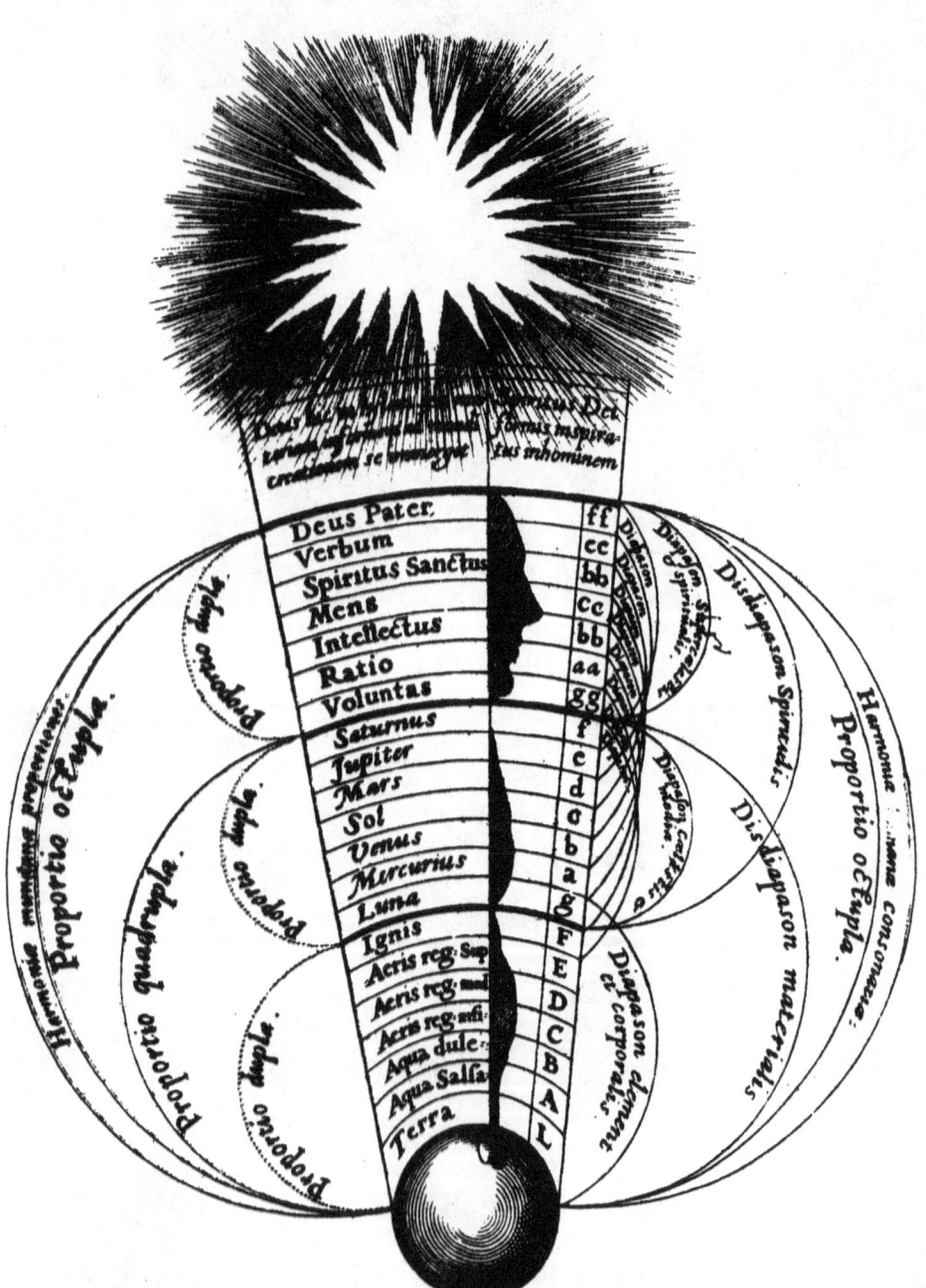

ASTROLOGICAL CHART OF MAN

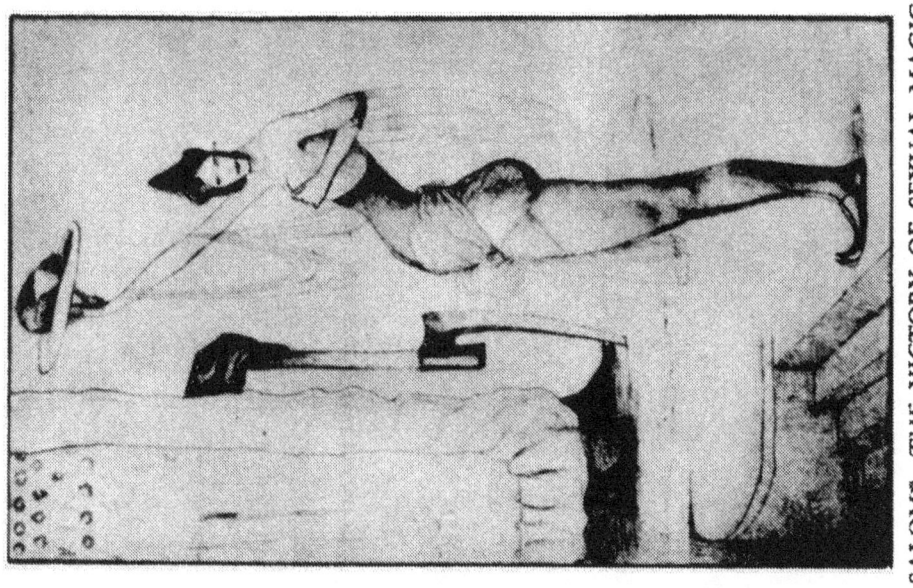

SALOME: THE VICTORY OF SEXUAL MAGIC

SELF-PORTRAIT OF AN ARTIST BESET BY DEMONS

ABOMINATIONS OF WITCHCRAFT

NIGHTMARE

SACRIFICES TO SATAN

THE LOVE POTION: *Tristan and Isolde*

WITCHES ANOINTING THE RITUAL GOAT

"DOUBLE, DOUBLE TOIL AND TROUBLE; FIRE BURN AND CAULDRON BUBBLE."
(Macbeth, IV, 1)

VAMPIRE AND VICTIMS

SATANIC TROPHIES

THE WITCHES' SABBATH

The witch god (with a light on his brow) and two companions are enthroned. Before them stands a child sacrifice or initiate. Elsewhere there are scenes of revelry and preparation of magic charms.

DEPARTURE FOR THE NOCTURNAL REVELS

NIGHT FLIGHT

www.ingramcontent.com/pod-product-compliance
Lightning Source LLC
Chambersburg PA
CBHW020942230426
43666CB00005B/133